TOTALLY UNMASKED ADULT AUTISM

8 Neurodiverse Tools To Safely
Unmask, Self-Advocate & Live With Joy
On The Autism Spectrum

Copyright © 2024 by LearnWell Books.

All rights reserved. No part of this publication may be reproduced, distributed, or transmitted in any form or by any means, including photocopying, recording, or other electronic or mechanical methods, without the prior written permission of the publisher, except in the case of brief quotations embodied in critical reviews and certain other noncommercial uses permitted by copyright law.

References to historical events, real people, or real places are often fictitious. In such cases, the names, characters, and places are products of the author's imagination. We do this where it's important to protect the privacy of people, places, and things.

689 Burke Rd
Camberwell Victoria 3124
Australia

www.LearnWellBooks.com

We're led by God. Our business is also committed to supporting kids' charities. At the time of printing, we have donated well over $100,000 to enable mentoring services for underprivileged children. By choosing our books, you are helping children who desperately need it. Thank you.

This Is Really Important.
It's a Sincere Thank You.

My name is Wayne, the founder of LearnWell.

My Dad put a book in my hands when I was 13. It was written by Zig Ziglar and it changed the course of my life. Since then, it's been books that have helped me get over breakups, learn how to be a good friend, study the lives of good people and books have been the source of my persistence through some pretty challenging times.

My purpose is now to return the favor. To create books that might be the turning point in the lives of people around the world, just like they've been for me. It's enough to almost bring me to tears to think of you holding this book, seeking information and wisdom from something that I've helped to create. I'm moved in a way that I can't fully explain.

We're a small and 'beyond-enthusiastic' team here at LearnWell. We're writers, editors, researchers, designers, formatters (oh ... and a bookkeeper!) who take your decision to learn with us incredibly seriously. We consider it a privilege to be part of your learning journey. Thank you for allowing us to join you.

If there's anything we did really well, anything we messed up, or anything AT ALL that we could do better, would you please write to us and tell us (like, right now!) We would love to hear from you!

readers@learnwellbooks.com

We're sending you our thanks, our love and our very best wishes.

Wayne
and the team at LearnWell Books.

WELCOME TO OUR COMMUNITY

"It's like a private online book club"

 Imagine if you could actually meet and talk with other readers of this book and share your experiences.

 Imagine if you could chat with the author or join them on a live Q&A!

 Imagine getting access to the author's notes and other exclusive, unpublished material.

You can do all of that and a lot more in the LearnWell Online Community!!

→ Download your **Workbook**
→ Chat directly with the author!
→ Meet and feel supported by other readers and their experiences.
→ Access additional, exclusive content about this topic and others.
→ Join our live Author Q&A sessions online.
→ Learn faster, make lasting changes, and have 10 times more fun!

This is part of our commitment to creating the best learning resources in the world.

Scan the QR code to get FREE access
www.learnwellbooks.com/unmask

**To my fellow, beautiful members
of the adult autistic community.**

I'm honored to join you as we make our way against the current, searching for our sense of belonging and for happiness.

We will all find it and rejoice.

CONTENTS

	Introduction	10

PART 1: A BETTER OUTLOOK   13

    1   **Embracing Autism**   14
           Shifting The Narrative From Disorder To Neurotype

    2   **The Unmasking Journey**   23
           Uncovering Your Truth And Honoring
           Your Unique Needs

PART 2: 8 TOOLS   33

    3   **Tool #1: A Strategic Approach To Stimming**   34
           Somatic Practices For Self-Regulation
           To Prevent Meltdowns And Shutdowns

    4   **Tool #2: Self-Accommodations**   60
           Easy Changes To Make The World
           More Comfortable For You

    5   **Tool #3: Prioritizing Joy The Autistic Way**   72
           The Importance Of Special Interests And
           Hobbies And How To Make Time For Them

6	**Tool #4: Journal Activities That Span The Spectrum**	81
	How To Make The Powerful Practice Of Journaling Work For You	
7	**Tool #5: The Game Of Executive Dysfunction**	98
	Using Play And Rewards For Improved Executive Functioning	
8	**Tool #6: Simple Steps To Self-Advocacy**	115
	How To Find Your Stronghold In Conversations And Relationships	
9	**Tool #7: Autistic Communication Skills**	129
	Building Connections And Confidence Without Losing Authenticity	
10	**Tool #8: Discover Your Sense Of Belonging**	144
	The Power Of Connecting Within The Autistic Community	
	Conclusion	154
	References	156

YOUR
WORKBOOK

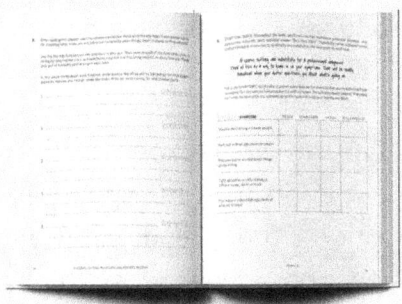

A shocking truth was discovered by a study done in 1987 – **people only remember 10% of what they read!**

That seems so discouraging.

But here's the **GOOD NEWS** – reading is **NEVER** a waste of time. As long as you do **one** important thing ...

The same study (by National Training Laboratories) shows that you will remember 90% of what you read when you **put your new knowledge into action**!

Here at LearnWell, we aim to create **the world's best learning resources**. So, we have included a highly engaging **Workbook** that helps you put your new knowledge into fun, practical action.

So, make sure you download your **FREE Workbook.** You'll find it located inside the **LearnWell Community.** Simply scan the QR code below for access.

Get your Workbook in the LearnWell Community
Scan the QR Code for access or go to:
www.learnwellbooks.com/unmask

INTRODUCTION

I'm autistic, and I see you.

The world can feel isolating and void of solutions for the uncomfortable and serious struggles we face. Left to many of the treatment options available, we may start to feel like we are only destined to survive when what we really want is to thrive.

We may wish to feel the vibrancy, ease, and comfort we see in so many people around us. But when we follow the same approaches that work for the majority and don't see the same result, it's easy to blame ourselves and feel fundamentally broken.

This is where I need you to know something. You are not the majority. The world was not designed to accommodate autistic needs. But that doesn't mean you're broken. It means the system is broken.

While we can't change the world overnight, you can certainly change your world. With a small mindset shift and the 8 tools within this book, you can feel empowered to live your life with more freedom, balance, and fun.

After a lifetime of trying to fit in, mask my needs, and "fix" myself, I was left in pieces. Mental illness felt normal; things that were important to me fell apart, and I had never felt more helpless. I struggled this way for years. Then came my autism diagnosis. It served to explain a lot of things, but it didn't change much at first.

Not until I realized I was working so hard trying to be something I'm simply not – normal.

Now, it's been years since I've fully embraced my differences. Autism used to feel like a burden, keeping me from achieving the life I strived for until I realized it was actually the key to unlocking the life that was meant for me. Everything changed when I stopped pushing against the current and simply allowed my life to flow around the rocks in the stream.

The solutions I offer throughout this book do not aim to change you. No, these solutions aim to encourage you to embrace your perfect autistic self and work with your traits to access something I believe we all deserve to experience—not autistic surviving but autistic thriving.

This book is divided into 2 Parts. Part 1 will start you off with an encouraging mindset shift that will help you embrace autism as a natural part of your neurology. It will then address the issue of suppressing autistic traits to fit in and how this book will encourage against that.

When you're ready, you will move on to Part 2, which includes 8 tools to thriving as an autistic adult. They include:

- Tool 1: A research-backed movement practice to enhance the impact of self-regulating behaviors like stimming, plus 15 accessible exercises to try straight away.

- Tool 2: Tips on supporting your own needs by meeting the intensity of the world in the middle.

- Tool 3: Reasons why joy is a vital autistic need and how you can prioritize it.

- Tool 4: Ways to make the highly effective practice of journaling work for you, including 10 autism-friendly journal exercises.

- Tool 5: Fun changes you can make to improve your executive functioning and get more done every day.

- Tool 6: How to find the confidence to advocate for yourself and keep yourself safe in an often dangerous world.

- Tool 7: A guide to autistic communication skills, including how to stay connected without crossing your own social boundaries.

- Tool 8: Everything you need to know about making like-minded connections as an adult within the autistic community.

Between coping with meltdowns and shutdowns, allowing more joy into your life, and so much more, let this book, and the LearnWell Community, empower you to create a life that works for you.  My heart and soul went into this book, and I can only wish that it reaches you in the way that you truly need. So, if you're ready to start thriving, turn the page and meet me in Chapter 1.

Love, Rose.

PART 1

A BETTER OUTLOOK

1

EMBRACING AUTISM

Shifting The Narrative From Disorder To Neurotype

"Our identities make us who we are, and all aspects of our identities are important, including (maybe even specifically) our disabilities."

— Chloé Hayden

Sipping the orange juice that came with my breakfast order, I watched the planes land through the airport window. I'd left my sunglasses at home, so the glare bouncing off the bright, low-hanging clouds burned my eyes. Already feeling at my limit for sensory exposure, things took a turn when the next flight announcement echoed through the noisy restaurant.

Like a short circuit through my brain's wiring, a meltdown began to pulse through me. The clothes on my back turned to barbed wire. My dad's hand on my shoulder, in an attempt to comfort me, felt like a claw pressing into me. My sister's "Are you okay?" sounded like a riddle without an answer. I stood up, grabbed my bag, and ran out the door past many concerned onlookers.

Outside, the sky began to close in on me. Wanting so badly to hide away, I stood around the corner and did my best to self-soothe without attracting too much attention. My hands flapped up and down, and I rocked gently on my feet. This kept things from worsening, but all I could do was wait it out until we could leave.

My dad came out, confirming that my sister was now boarding her flight, and we left. Knowing I had to endure a full day in the city, feeling wired in every way, I made a simple decision that changed my life. I did something I was always too embarrassed to do before having grown up undiagnosed. I purchased my first pair of noise-canceling headphones and wore them in public for the rest of the day.

It took me years to fully accept the news after holding the diagnostic papers that read: Autism Spectrum Disorder. But in that moment, feeling the intensity of the world fade, I embraced it. This was the beginning of a change in my story. A change that turned autism into something I wanted to understand deeply, embrace fully, and advocate for.

I won't say that I never have meltdowns anymore, that my sensory issues are resolved, or that I'm suddenly living the life of a normal, high-functioning, allistic person. Being autistic comes with many complex challenges. But I will say this:

I wouldn't erase my autism for anything in the world. The sensitive, smart, and silly sides to me are all sides so tightly interlaced with autistic traits that removing my autism would unravel me. My autistic traits are not separate from me. They are me. And there isn't a world that could exist without autism where I could exist too.

After applying what I'm going to share with you throughout this book, things definitely improved. Life is now filled with more joy and connection than I ever thought was possible for me. When I look in the mirror, I can smile and truly love who I am. I'm no longer trying to be something or someone I'm not. I'm living my life in a way that is perfectly normal for me, an adult who has chosen a new narrative about her autism.

Although autism is diagnosed with very clinical, symptomatic language, it is not a disease. We live in a world where anything other than the cookie-cutter mold is seen as less than or broken. But we are not broken. We are not less than. Our disabilities do not define us. We define them.

Autism is not a disorder acquired from mistreatment, injury, or bad parenting. It's an integral part of every autistic person's brain.

Our disabilities do not define us. We define them.

We are not people with the disorder of autism. We are autistic. Simply and beautifully autistic.

DEFINING ASD AND ADDRESSING THE CURRENT NARRATIVE

Before we can go any further, let's dive into the definition of autism as it currently stands. Autism Spectrum Disorder, known as ASD, is the all-encompassing diagnosis received for autism of all support levels. It is difficult to define because the spectrum is so vast, and each autistic person experiences autism uniquely. But imagine the various traits of autism are on a color wheel, and each autistic person has their own variation of traits.

Autism is classified as a neurological and developmental disorder impacting the way we socialize, communicate, learn, and behave.[1] Included in an ASD diagnosis is a supports need label. There are three levels:

- Level 1: Requires support.
- Level 2: Requires substantial support.
- Level 3: Requires very substantial support.

However, I want to make something very clear. While support labels were likely put in place with the best intentions, and they do aim to serve a purpose, they fail us in a very big way. The entire autistic narrative often does. All autistic people with ASD labeled as "higher functioning" or "low support needs" still stand the chance to experience times in life when more substantial support is required.

In day-to-day life, all levels of autistic people may experience moments of functioning and feeling good. Still, only those labeled as level 3 or "lower functioning" may be eligible for adequate support when they aren't functioning as well.

Support labels make it easier to overlook those with lower support needs in times of struggle. They are given as a once-off label during the time of diagnosis. And if you're anything like me, no day is ever the same. Support needs vary so much that receiving a once-off label may later restrict you from getting the correct support.

This is just one example of how the current narrative surrounding autism is not serving the autistic community as it should. And there are many more.

For example, trained professionals are able to diagnose ASD in children as young as 2 years old. Still, so many of us slip through the cracks and are only diagnosed later in life if we're lucky because the stereotype often doesn't include females or black, indigenous, and people of color (BIPOC) communities.[2] Relying on a more stereotypical view of autism leaves large portions of the autistic community without proper support.

There are also many misconceptions running the narrative around autism, such as "autistic people lack empathy." While autistic traits and empathy are tightly linked, the differences in empathy are more of a unique disequilibrium.[3] A disequilibrium of empathy suggests that autistic people may experience empathy differently rather than simply being at a deficit.

Unfortunately, there are grave consequences that follow a narrative that often isn't helpful. From our heightened risk of being bullied or abused to our limited treatment options, living in a world where feeling misunderstood is largely normal comes with a big price.

When autistic people only make up 1% of the population but 11% of all suicides, we need to start asking questions. When 66% of autistic adults have considered taking their lives, alarm bells should ring. And when children on the spectrum are 28 times more likely to have suicidal thoughts, it's clear change is due.[4]

Although the reasoning behind these statistics is not yet clear, it takes very deep unhappiness and prolonged suffering to want to take your life. I know this because I'm a part of these statistics. After years of trauma and bullying followed by a severe lack of understanding or treatment, at just 16 years old, I couldn't take it anymore. I tried to take my life.

Upon confiding in the thousands of autistic adults in my online community, over 80% felt that the general narrative around autism was, at best, unhelpful, with 1 out of 3 claiming it was harmful and ableist.

The autistic narrative needs to change. But it isn't just the responsibility of the world to accept us more. It's also our responsibility to accept ourselves. We need to shed any form of narrative that is limiting and embrace our autistic selves unapologetically.

EMBRACING NEURODIVERGENCE

The narrative I'd like to reinforce, along with a growing portion of the adult autistic community, starts with the term: neurodivergence. Created by autistic sociologist Judy Singer, who wanted to find an alternative to deficit-based language, neurodivergence is where autism is accepted as a naturally occurring difference in brain structure rather than a disorder to be eradicated.[5]

Claiming and embracing your neurodivergence is a powerful way to accept yourself. It allows you to make decisions based on what works for you rather than how you can change to fit the standards of society. If your brain is different by nature, going against that only serves to hold you back. But embracing that empowers you to change your life for the better.

I will encourage you to self-advocate throughout this book. I'd like you to be open to letting go of any limitations put on you by others or yourself. Be open to the fact that you are likely more capable than you know. You can live your life the way that you not only want to but need to.

Autistic people are different. That means you need to be open to adjusting the way you do things to work for you. You need to be open to shifting the way you accept, embrace, and live as your autistic self. This is not about bypassing the medical system but rather understanding that research about the lived autistic experience is extremely limited. You need to learn to trust yourself and form your own understanding of what autism means to you. You need to stop seeing yourself as broken and start seeing yourself as perfectly autistic.

Take a moment now to think about what autism means to you. How does it impact who you are? We spend so much time focusing on our struggles and deficits in comparison to people who aren't on the spectrum. But there's much more to autism than the negative labels placed on us.

For example, you might have been told that you lack empathy because you don't show it with the "appropriate" facial expressions. Meanwhile, in your heart, you know that you feel deeply for others and show empathy in different ways. You might have been told that you lack social skills because you're very blunt and straightforward. But who decided that being blunt was negative? Maybe the clarity and fierceness that you communicate with is actually more practical.

Every autistic person will experience being on the spectrum differently. Understanding your experience can help you embrace your differences and know which areas you may need the most support. When you're ready, there is an exercise waiting for you in your Workbook with a few questions you can answer to prime yourself for full self-acceptance.

The first step on this journey is to accept that you are autistic and be open to letting it show. The next step is to fully embrace it unapologetically. Many of us have been taught by fear to hide our autism and camouflage ourselves for the comfort of others. If you're ready to say screw that, then turn the page, and let's start the process of unmasking in whatever way you need to. You deserve to thrive just as much as anybody, and – from one autistic person to another – it is absolutely possible.

2

THE UNMASKING JOURNEY

Uncovering Your Truth And Honoring Your Unique Needs

"Masking is effectively holding your breath; the regulation you need to occur does not occur, and eventually, you either have to breathe or pass out."

– Kieran Rose

Growing up, getting hit for bad behavior was normal. My mom, overwhelmed and misinformed, often lashed out at me. Sometimes, I was doing things I wasn't supposed to, but other times, the pain came without knowing why.

Holding my mom's hand as we walked through the mall, I quickly became fidgety. The lights buzzed loudly above the sound of people streaming in and out of stores. There were colorful advertisements, products, and labels everywhere. And I could sense a change in my mom that I now recognize as embarrassment.

I felt her hand grip the back of my neck as she glared down at me. I didn't understand what I was doing wrong. The fidgeting continued. It was as if the movements made the world quieter. Then, out of nowhere, she dragged me into the bathroom corridor and "Whack!"

It didn't take long for me to understand that fidgeting was "wrong," even though it made me feel better. The one thing I could do naturally to self-regulate wasn't safe. Fitting in was better and I had to learn how to do it quickly, or else.

This was the beginning of my masking journey – my journey of learning to hide anything about me that was seen as different. It was unknowingly the start of hiding my autistic traits from the world. And it's part of the reason why I managed to go undiagnosed for 25 years despite struggling so immensely.

Most people mask from time to time. It's what we do when we don't feel great but have to show up cheerfully to a work meeting anyway. It's the moments we choose to present ourselves in a more palatable way and hide our truth. However, autistic people who mask often take this to new levels. They camouflage who they really are rather than just how they feel.

Autistic masking is when an autistic person suppresses their autistic traits, hides their struggles, and puts on a show of what they believe is considered typical. It's when fidgeting would help them calm down, but they choose discomfort to please others. It's when they're passionate about the topic of discussion but choose to keep quiet to avoid being a know-it-all. It's when they do what it takes to fit in to avoid bullying, isolation, or abuse. Masking is a survival technique for autistic people, but in the long term, it doesn't do us any favors.

WHY MASKING HURTS US

Even though it may seem harmless to want to fit in, suppressing autistic traits leaves autistic people dysregulated. It's exhausting. Masking effectively in social settings requires an advanced level of hypervigilance. This can include forcing eye contact, actively observing and copying facial expressions, suppressing self-soothing behaviors, and mimicking typical body language, all while trying to pay attention and keep up with a conversation.

This level of masking may feel beneficial in the short term as we experience improved social responses and belonging, but the long-term impact may be detrimental. Autistic masking has proven to increase signs of anxiety and depression, decrease our sense of identity, and leave us at risk for autistic burnout, something that may take years to overcome.[6]

Masking can hide our authentic selves so well that we lose sight of it. The trouble is that truly thriving requires authenticity. It's very difficult to feel satisfied in a life that isn't built around who you really are.

Of course, not all autistic people mask. Many autistic people who have perhaps grown up diagnosed at a young age or who have not undergone therapies that reinforce suppression of autistic traits will likely not mask at all. Each one of our experiences will be unique. But for those of us who have been forced to hide our true selves out of safety, indoctrination, or a desire to fit in, we may need to unmask in order to feel our best.

There are many reasons why it may not be safe to fully unmask, such as if you are in an environment where differences could lead to mistreatment. However, I will encourage you to unmask to a degree that you are able to or to find times when you can fully unmask safely.

The objective is not to expose parts of yourself that you aren't comfortable with but rather to discover any unmet needs you may have hiding beneath the surface. You may:

- Find new ways to regulate yourself in times of stress.
- Meet parts of yourself that have been hidden since childhood.
- Learn what you really want and need out of life.
- Salvage energy stores normally used for masking.

- Experience a sense of ease and self-acceptance you've never had access to before.

Unmasking is a necessary step to living a fulfilling life as an autistic adult. Even if you choose to only unmask when you are home alone, it's important to find spaces where you can be yourself, regulate yourself, and honor your needs.

LEARNING TO UNMASK

Many of the tools you will learn in this book will require you to work *with* your autistic traits. As you learned in the previous chapter, this starts with self-acceptance. Unmasking is not always a simple process. It can take time and a slow unlearning of the narrative that leads you to masking. However, 3 things you can do right now to start unmasking include:

1. Practice Self-Compassion

Unmasking may require you to challenge societal norms and confront false beliefs about who you are allowed to be. It will likely include moments of discomfort as you expand the boundaries that you have established based on your experiences as an autistic person.

For example, if you have been taught that stimming, the self-stimulatory behavior that allows so many autistic people to regulate themselves, is embarrassing to do in public, regardless of how dysregulated you are, then allowing yourself to stim when needed may feel like a challenge.

Changing what has been the norm for you, even something that may be harmful, could invoke self-doubt and criticism as you navigate challenging emotions and bypass false beliefs. This is where self-compassion is going to be your greatest ally along your unmasking journey.

You can practice self-compassion by:

- Being kind and patient with yourself along this journey.
- Facing criticism and self-doubt with an encouraging and understanding inner dialogue.
- Tackling challenges gently without pushing yourself too far or too fast.
- Respecting your boundaries by giving yourself permission to take breaks or slow down.
- Checking in with yourself regularly throughout this process to make sure you are regulated.

Even though unmasking may feel like a massive relief, it can also be a jarring experience if you have come to rely on your mask for social interactions. If you start to feel uncomfortable or unsure of whether unmasking is the right choice, come back to its core goal – living your life in a more authentic way. Even if it's only when you are alone or safe to do so, life is so much more fulfilling when you don't suppress your true needs and nature.

Self-compassion will help you find the courage to work through the challenges of discovering who you really are. When you're ready, take a moment to visit your Workbook and complete the exercise that is waiting for you. It will help you find a sense of self-compassion right now in less than 5 minutes.

2. Address Any Internalized Ableism

Our world is largely designed without differences in mind. There is a common social prejudice against disabled people that often leads to discrimination. This is called ableism. Ableism is when people with disabilities are seen as less valuable or less important than the general population.

There are varying degrees of ableism, and most of society has been guilty of it at some point. It includes misconceptions, harmful stereotypes, and generalizations about people with disabilities.[7] Some examples include when buildings fail to offer wheelchair-friendly entrances, when a teenager calls their friend "mentally challenged," or when mothers of typical children refuse to let their kids play with the non-verbal autistic child.

Any kind of discomfort or judgment that comes when someone sees a disabled person is often born from ableism. But even disabled people can be ableists. We can internalize the ableism we have experienced and start to see our disability as "wrong." We can start to *feel* less than we are because of an internalized belief that we are less. We can mask our disabled traits in an attempt to hide something that should be seen as natural.

Do you see where I'm going with this? Autistic masking may be a form of internalized ableism if you have been brought up in a society or culture where autism is seen as inherently bad. So, to be able to unmask, it's important that you address any forms of ableism you may have internalized throughout your life. Examples of internalized ableism for autistic people may include:

- Feeling uncomfortable around openly autistic people.
- Punishing yourself for showing autistic traits.
- Experiencing shame after an autistic meltdown.
- Masking your wants and needs to fit in or satisfy others.
- Using ableist language like "retard" or "cripple."
- Wanting to get rid of or "cure" your autism.

If you have been masking your autistic traits, it's possible you have some degree of internalized ableism. Allow yourself to face it, address it, and let it go to help you find a deeper sense of self-acceptance. If internalized ableism is a contributing factor to your need to mask, addressing it will make unmasking more appealing and comfortable for you.

3. Commit To Authenticity

Authenticity aligns your actions, choices, and values with who you are, creating a more fulfilling and happy life. Committing to authenticity will naturally begin the unmasking process.

Unmasking is nothing more than embracing your authentic autistic self and allowing yourself to live as that person. This can mean many things, but most importantly, it should mean creating a life that is more balanced and tuned into your unique needs and desires.

A commitment to authenticity means that you are willing to live your life the way you need to, regardless of how different that may look in comparison to others or your current perception of what a successful adult life should look like. Make this commitment now and remember it as you continue on through the next eight chapters.

Your commitment to living a more authentic life is going to carry you through each chapter and allow you to fully apply what you learn with space for something new. So, if you're ready to find new ways to thrive in a wildly busy world, then turn the page now and meet me in Chapter 3, where you will learn the first tool in your autistic adulting toolbox.

PART 2

8 TOOLS

TOOL #1:
A STRATEGIC APPROACH TO STIMMING

Somatic Practices For Self-Regulation To Prevent Meltdowns And Shutdowns

"All responses to the world take place within our bodies."

– Gloria Anzaldua

It had been a bad day—one of those days where your sleeve catches the door handle on your way out. Every little thing that could go wrong did. It was the kind of day that would usually end in a full-blown meltdown or shutdown. I could feel the tension in my body rising on the ride home, and my mind was racing. All I wanted was to get home and cope with the aftermath.

A few months before, I would have reached the door, closed it behind myself, and crumbled. I would've been too exhausted to shower, cook a proper meal, or even do something I enjoyed. A long, hard day like this one would've ended with me straight in bed, drowning out the noise in my head with mindless TV.

But I'd learned a lot since then.

I reached my front door, took a deep breath, and went inside. I could feel the tears welling up, and I acknowledged them. I allowed them to come quietly as I walked over to the special corner in my house. This was a place I had created where I was safe to process the day's emotions. It was a sacred space where I came to breathe, cry, and move my body the way I needed to.

Lying down on my mat, pressing a pillow to my face, I screamed. The frustration roared out, muted by the dense stuffing. The tears stopped, but a sense of uneasiness still crawled through my body. Closing my eyes, I knew this energy needed to be released, and there was only one way to do it – through movement.

So, hugging the pillow to my chest, I used my feet to instigate a rocking motion throughout my body. The repetitive sensation lulled me, and a deep sigh escaped my mouth. The uneasiness began to still, my mind quietened, and all I knew at that moment was the consistency of the rocking sensation. After about 20 minutes on the mat, the badness of the day was washed away, and I felt capable of carrying on. I could get up, take a slow shower, and muster a decent meal.

Movement is magic for autistic people.

But I'm not just talking about the way exercise is good for you. No, this is the kind of movement that unwinds emotional build-up at its core. It stimulates the highly intelligent system in our bodies that allows us to rest deeply and fully. And it's something that most autistic people have built in like some form of natural, self-regulating tool we come wired with.

A need for self-stimulatory behavior, or stimming, is one of the most common autistic traits. It's the hand-flapping, body rocking, repetitive vocalizations, and more that you might come to expect from an unmasked autistic person experiencing a strong emotion. But there is something that works in a very similar way. A practice that uses movement to regulate the nervous system, process emotions, and even work through trauma. It's known as Somatic Practice.

As your first tool for autistic thriving, I will show you how to use somatic practice as a form of strategic stimming, whether you are someone who naturally stims or not. I will explain why it's important to stim and how you can do it in a way that works for you. Every autistic person has unique needs but often similar struggles. So even if you don't engage in usual autistic stimming, you won't want to skip this.

Movement is magic for autistic people.

Stimming and somatic practice have very similar benefits, which I'll get into soon. But one of the ways that makes them both so perfect for autistic people is their ability to soothe the mind with the body. They both act on the mind-body connection, something at the root of many common autistic struggles, like proprioception issues, emotional overwhelm, sensory difficulties, and more. But let's start by understanding stimming and why movement is an autistic necessity.

SELF-STIMULATORY BEHAVIOR

Any movement or sound you make on repeat to regulate yourself in times of stress, anxiety, or sensory overwhelm can be a stim. But stims can also serve as an outlet for intense positive emotions. Anything from jumping up and down to tapping a pen against your desk, stims can take on any form or level of intensity. What sets them apart from other movements is their purpose. They usually don't have any other purpose other than to serve as an outlet for energy, helping to regulate your nervous system.

Stimming is also not exclusive to autism. Various other conditions, like anxiety, could cause stimming behaviors. And sometimes, it's simply our natural human expression of emotions. You might stim without even knowing it, for example, repeatedly fixing your hair during a stressful meeting, tapping your foot impatiently while you wait for your bus, or whistling to express your joy.

However, in the context of someone with autism, stimming may simply be more of a necessity.[8] It forms a vital part of our emotional processing, which remains a common struggle for most autistic people throughout our lives.

Where neurotypical people – people without any neurodivergence – can often regulate themselves throughout the day without much thought, autistic people may need a more rigorous and strategic approach. Autism impacts the nervous system greatly, leaving autistic people more susceptible to problems with anxiety, panic attacks, and depression – all problems that often spur from nervous system dysregulation and problems processing emotions or difficult situations.[9]

EMOTIONS AND THE AUTISTIC MIND

The differences in our nervous systems can lead to meltdowns and shutdowns for many autistic people, often lasting into adulthood. Meltdowns and shutdowns are two sides of the same coin. They are opposite reactions to a sympathetic nervous system response. This is the part of the nervous system responsible for our "fight," "flight," or "freeze" response to danger. However, it can activate more easily in autistic people due to excessive stimuli, anxiety, or emotional overwhelm.

Meltdowns are a dysregulated "fight" response that can induce feelings of rage, loss of control, heightened anxiety or emotion, excessive stimming, and even self-injury. Shutdowns are a dysregulated "freeze" response, inducing a sense of emotional numbness, physical slowness or stillness, a desire to isolate, and sometimes an inability to move or talk at all.[10]

The autistic mind has been studied immensely without any solid conclusions drawn as to why it is so sensitive and unique. However, The Intense World Theory has unified all current hypotheses around autistic neurobiology. It proposes that the autistic mind experiences the world so intensely with increased sensory sensitivity, social withdrawal, repetitive behavior, and potential for exceptional talents because of its hyper-reactivity and hyper-plasticity.[11]

There are many regions in an autistic brain that are more active than a typical brain, including areas responsible for fear processing. This gives us valuable insight into our ability to process stimuli we perceive as dangerous, including overwhelming emotions. Our brains process more information at any given time, with studies showing an average increase in information of 41% at rest in autistic children.[12]

This is why it is vital for autistic adults to actively implement some form of emotional processing to stay on top of the mental overload we may experience. If you want to do more, feel better, and stay regulated, you have to meet this constant need. Stimming is a built-in processing system many of us use to help regulate and express this excess.

For example, people who stim openly might express intense joy by jumping up and down with flapping hands—also fondly referred to as happy hands. Some autistic people may have a go-to stim that they do regularly to stay focused and relaxed, such as repeating a favorite catchphrase, tapping their fingers, or rocking their bodies from side to side. But most commonly, many of us may stim excessively during times of stress to release that excess energy.

Whether you stim or not, taking time to regulate your nervous system, process excess emotions, and simply express yourself will help lighten the mental load that naturally comes with living in an intense world. Rather than waiting until things become too much, you can create a space where you safely and consciously allow yourself to stim. This is where I'd like to introduce you to somatic practice.

THE POWER OF SOMATIC PRACTICE FOR AUTISM

Now that you understand the intricacies of the autistic mind and how our processing abilities—both emotional and physiological—could be linked to nervous system dysregulation, somatic practice will make a lot of sense. It's all about using your body to regulate your mind through movements, both intuitive and structured. It's a body-up approach to mental well-being.

Somatic practice, also known as somatic experiencing, is a movement-based practice proven to regulate the nervous system, release tension, and process trauma. It is based on the philosophy that humans have the same trauma-processing response as animals. This is the natural tremoring mechanism of the body that causes the body to quite literally "shake off" trauma or distress. However, a similar response can be accessed in many ways, using many forms of movement, including making sounds.

Because of the improved mind-body connection that comes with regular somatic practice, there are many additional benefits that make somatics excellent for autistic people. For example, two of the most common problems that form part of the autistic experience include proprioception issues, when the brain struggles to process the body in space, and poor interoception, when the brain struggles to interpret natural body cues like hunger or a full bladder. These two things can drastically improve with a stronger mind-body connection.[13]

Improved proprioception can help with balance, coordination, and an improved understanding of your body in space. Improved interoception can help with better emotional recognition and regulation and an improved ability to understand your body's needs.

Somatic practice aims to improve your well-being in a holistic way, allowing you to use it for multiple purposes. It can help you to:

- Identify early indicators of nervous system dysregulation to better prevent meltdowns, shutdowns, burnout, and excessive stress.

- Gradually release built-up tension in a more comforting and controlled way to avoid destructive behavior or unnecessary emotional distress.

- Develop a deeper sense of self-awareness to cultivate personal agency, confidence in decision-making, and independence.

- Notice signals in the body and mind that indicate relaxation or emotional stabilization so you can lean into them quicker and feel them solidify.

- Improve sensory integration, allowing you to better process and regulate sensory information to reduce overload and increase comfort in challenging environments.

It's also possible and recommended to choose specific somatic exercises that align with your needs. Unlike many other forms of exercise or movement-based practices, somatic practice is very flexible. You can create a somatic practice that works for you. There is nothing rigid about it.

The types of somatic exercises available vary so much that there is something to suit anyone's needs and comfort levels. For example, if you hate stretching, stick to rocking, wriggling, or shaking exercises. If too much movement feels jarring for you, lean into the stillness, breathing, or mindfulness side of things. If you love to make noise, try humming practices. The nervous system is a highly adaptive, multi-faceted system that can be impacted in many ways.

Autism often comes with difficulty understanding the intensity of life. But practicing somatic exercises regularly allows you to tune into yourself and really feel your way through life. It also allows you to better identify what you need at any given time so you can care for yourself how you deserve.

I'm going to give you some specific examples of somatic exercises that may work to improve some of the most common struggles autistic adults face. As you read, think about the areas in your life where you experience the most difficulties. At the end of this chapter, you will have the opportunity to create an easy somatic routine that you can do daily. I'd like to encourage you to have an open mind and take note of which exercises resonate with you as we continue.

SOMATIC EXERCISES FOR AUTISM

It's important to note that somatic exercises are adjustable to accommodate your needs and abilities. Most standing exercises can be adjusted to work in a seated position, and many can be completed lying down. Try the exercises that work for you, and feel free to adjust them to meet your needs and requirements if necessary.

I've chosen exercises that work well for various autistic struggles to help you recognize which ones may suit your unique challenges. This section contains 15 exercises split into subsections for various struggles. If you enjoy them and would like to expand your somatic practice, you can find 35 more exercises in our book Somatic Exercises For Nervous System Regulation. As you continue, remember to take note of the exercises you feel drawn to.

Meltdown Prevention

These somatic exercises are designed to help release intense bursts of energy, including rage, frustration, and emotional overwhelm. They work to relieve the "fight" response from your nervous system and bring you back to baseline.

Pillow Slams

This is a simple exercise that you can use to safely release the urge to lash out, throw things, or hit something. You can do this in the midst of a meltdown or just before to help you release the energy before it becomes too much. I recommend having a designated pillow that you save for this exercise, but any pillow will do. To complete a pillow slam somatic exercise:

- Choose your pillow and hold it at either end firmly.

- Stand with your feet about hip-width apart with knees slightly bent.
- Grip the pillow and lift it above your head.
- Bring it down as hard as you can, letting it go so that it slams firmly against the ground.
- Pick the pillow up again, and repeat as necessary.

If you feel the need to shout or scream, you can also combine your pillow slam exercise with a scream into the pillow. Do this by taking a deep breath in, pushing the pillow to your face, and screaming into it to muffle the sound. When you're done, be gentle with yourself and quietly notice how you feel.

Expressive Movement

Emotions can move through our bodies in unexpected ways. Meltdowns are what happen when we don't feel safe to express ourselves, and the emotions, stress, or tension build up to the point of explosion. Expressing yourself when needed is a great way to avoid this build-up and create a stronger sense of resilience to stressors. Unrepressed expressive movement can help you express yourself without needing to overthink or analyze how you feel. To do it, simply:

- Find a quiet, comfortable place to stand.
- Put on music that aligns with how you feel to help you tune into your emotions and express yourself fully.
- Close your eyes if you're comfortable, and begin to move your body in any way that feels good.

- You can try shaking various limbs, jumping around, stomping your feet, swinging your arms, swaying your head, or whatever other movements feel good.

- Continue for a few minutes or as long as you feel you need to.

The goal of this exercise is to move your body in any way it needs to without judgment or worry of looking strange. Your body may require specific movements to release trapped or built-up emotions that may otherwise seem awkward, inappropriate, or embarrassing. Take this time to fully express yourself through movement without a care in the world. If you feel stuck and don't know where to start, shake out one limb at a time and then see what movements come next. Let your body lead the way.

Cathartic Breathing

When we start to become overwhelmed and our nervous system enters the fight-or-flight state, breathing is often one of the first things to change. It can become shallow and quickened, or we may even hold it in. Cathartic breathing is a quick and effective way to signal safety to your nervous system. All you need to do is:

- Find a quiet place to sit or lie down and close your eyes if you're comfortable.

- Place your left hand on your stomach and your right hand on your chest.

- Inhale deeply through your nose, pulling the air into your stomach. Aim to feel your left hand rise while your right hand stays mostly still.

- On the exhale, open your mouth and release the air in a big cathartic sigh with a long "Ah" sound. You can also groan or make whatever sound feels the most relieving.

- Repeat for 3-5 breaths.

If letting out a big sigh feels too overwhelming, you can also purse your lips like you're blowing on hot soup and slowly blow the exhale out. Allow the air escaping to make a sound so you can hear the air releasing for a similar cathartic effect.

Breaking Out Of Shutdown

Being stuck in a shutdown can be an unnerving experience. You may feel detached, numb, or still on the outside and chaotic on the inside. Whatever a shutdown feels like for you, it is generally the "freeze" nervous system response in action. However, you can help break yourself out of this state by activating your nervous system in various ways. This is when stillness practices are not advised, and gentle nervous system stimulation is best.

VOO Breathing

Activating the Vagus Nerve in the nervous system is one of the easiest ways to trigger homeostasis in the body.[14] This nerve runs throughout the entire body but is easiest to access around the vocal cords. VOO breathing activates the vagus nerve by vibrating the vocal cords and stimulating the vagus nerve. To try VOO breathing:

- Find a private place to sit, stand, or lie down.

- If you're comfortable, close your eyes to increase body awareness.

- Inhale deeply through your nose, expanding your stomach.

- For the entire exhale, say the word "VOO" slowly in a deep tone.

- Breathe normally for a moment and notice any shifts in your body and mind.

- Repeat 3-5 times, breathing normally in between each for a moment.

The deeper and more steady your "VOO" is, the better it will vibrate the vocal cords, stimulating the vagus nerve. More ways to stimulate the vagus nerve include humming, singing, and gargling.

Gentle Dancing

Shutdowns make your body want to be still in an attempt to protect you from danger. But being too still can prolong a shutdown. Low-intensity movement will activate the nervous system in a way that signals safety to your body. A great form of low-intensity movement that can both bring you out of shutdown and uplift your mood is gentle dancing. This is when you:

- Put on some light, relaxing, or happy music.

- Slowly and gently move your body in any way that feels good.

- Movements can include gentle swaying, rocking quietly from side to side, stretching your body, lightly moving your arms and legs, or any other slow and gentle movements.

- Continue to dance gently for as long as you like, closing your eyes to feel your way back into your body.

Use this exercise to bring your awareness back into your body in a gentle and uplifting way. If music doesn't feel good, you can do this exercise without it, tuning into the sound of your breath instead.

Grounding

Shutdowns can pull you into your head and out of your environment or body. A great way to bring yourself back to the present moment and stabilize yourself is through grounding somatic practices. Grounding requires you to gently bring your awareness to your senses. To do this:

- Take a deep breath in and bring your awareness to the things you can see in your environment. Pick 5 things and name them to yourself.

- Now, as you continue to breathe, bring your awareness to your body and focus on any sensations you can feel. Pick 4 sensations or objects you can feel, such as the ground beneath your feet, the fluffy blanket over your lap, the breeze on your face, and the sensation of rubbing your thumb against your hand.

- Next, focus on 3 sounds you can hear in your environment. This could be anything from the birds chirping, music playing, people talking, or anything else around you.

- See if you can pick up on 2 aromas you can smell. If there aren't any specific aromas around you, you can pick up things that smell good, like a piece of fruit, your cup of tea, or even a pet.

- Finally, find something that you can taste and pull your awareness into the experience as much as possible. Choosing something sour, like lemon, or something very sweet can help increase the grounding effects.

- When you're ready, bring your awareness to your breathing, and finish the exercise with a few long, slow, and deep breaths.

Improved Proprioception

Most somatic exercises will work to improve proprioception by increasing your mind-body connection. But some exercises will be more focused on proprioception issues like balance and coordination, such as:

Single Leg Stands

This is a simple exercise that works to improve your balance. You can complete it during your active somatic practice or at any time throughout the day. Simply:

- Set a timer on your phone and aim for about 30 seconds or more per leg.

- Stand on one leg, resting your lifted foot on your ankle or lower leg.

- Balance on one leg for as long as you can and switch to the other side.

- Repeat the exercise for up to 2 minutes, using the timer to track your progress.

Don't be discouraged if you can't balance for 30 seconds on each leg. Balance can improve relatively quickly when practiced regularly. If you practice often and would like an extra challenge, close your eyes at the end of each session and aim for an extra 10 seconds of balancing per leg.

Mindful Walking

Mindful walking can improve proprioception by increasing your bodily awareness as you move through space. It can also work to ground you in the present and keep you relaxed. To walk mindfully:

- Stand up straight and take a deep breath.

- Bring your awareness to the soles of your feet, preferably standing barefoot.

- Slowly lift one foot and take a step forward, focusing your awareness on every sensation and movement that entails.

- Repeat on the other foot, then continue moving forward, keeping your awareness locked into the experience.

- Now bring your awareness to the swaying of your arms. Notice how they move in relation to your steps, particularly how the right arm moves forward in tandem with the left foot and vice versa.

- Continue for a few minutes or as long as you feel comfortable.

You can practice mindful walking any time you need to move around or walk somewhere. Simply bring your awareness to your body and notice the sensations of walking.

Elephant Yoga Pose

Yoga is an ancient somatic practice with a host of benefits for both mind and body. There are hundreds of poses to choose from, but this yoga exercise is a fun way to bring your awareness to your body while engaging the mind in a relaxing visualization. To enjoy the elephant yoga pose:

- Stand with your feet hip-width apart and bend your knees if needed.
- Bend at the hips, letting your hands hang down to the floor.
- Place one hand on top of the other and interlace your fingers.
- Imagine that you are an elephant, and your arms are your trunk.
- Allow your arms to become heavy as you sway them left and right like an elephant would swing its trunk.

You can enjoy this yoga pose for a few moments or as long as you'd like. It not only gives your entire body a nice stretch, but it is also a fun way to tune into your body and improve your balance and coordination.

Emotional Recognition

Understanding our emotions is a common autistic struggle that leaves us at risk for emotional build-up. It can feel like we are experiencing an intense emotion but without an understanding of what the emotion is or how to best work through it. Somatic exercises can help improve emotional recognition and give us new insights into how our bodies experience different emotions so we can feel empowered to cope more effectively.

Body Scan Exercise

The purpose of a body scan is simply to notice. With a sense of curiosity, noticing the various sensations throughout your body while experiencing an emotion, even the uncomfortable ones, can give you valuable insights into your body's emotional processing. To do a body scan:

- Choose a quiet, comfortable place where you can sit or lie down.
- Close your eyes and center your awareness with a couple of deep breaths..
- Slowly, scan your awareness up through your body, from your feet to the top of your head, noticing any sensations associated with how you feel. For example, warmth in your face for anger or tightness in the stomach for anxiety.
- As you scan, just notice the sensations without judgment or avoidance. Use this as an opportunity to understand the emotions better and make space for them.
- When you reach the top of your head, take a moment to notice how your body as a whole feels then slowly wiggle your fingers and toes, moving your body gently and opening your eyes.

Breath Awareness

Changes in your breathing patterns can be a vital signal to what emotion is about to move through you. But you can also change your breathing to help regulate uncomfortable emotions. Breath awareness will help you better recognize these changes and feel confident managing them with the help of intentional breathing. To practice breath awareness:

- Close your eyes and bring your awareness to your breathing.

- Don't try to change it for a moment; simply notice it and recognize the pattern associated with whatever emotion you're feeling. For example, quick, shallow breaths are associated with anxiety, heavy breaths might be associated with anger, and holding your breath could mean overwhelm.

- Slowly start to take conscious control of your breathing, deepening and slowing your breath gently.

- Notice the difference in your body now as your relaxed breathing signals safety to your body.

This exercise can be part of your daily practice to reinforce using the breath to understand and regulate emotions. But it's also great to use in the spur of the moment.

Guided Imagery

This is an exploratory exercise that can help you identify emotions by learning which sensations go with which emotions. Be prepared to feel uncomfortable, as this exercise works by recalling emotions you'd like to explore. If you're nervous, you can ask a trusted friend, family member, or therapist to be with you. To try this exercise:

- Find a comfortable place to sit or lie down and close your eyes.

- Breathe deeply and slowly as you imagine yourself in a peaceful place of your choice. Notice any sensations of ease and safety that come up in your body.

- When you're ready, recall any emotion you'd like to explore, such as sadness, anger, or happiness. Think of the last time you experienced the emotion.

- Notice how the emotion manifests in your body, including how it feels, where you feel it, and any sensations that arise with it.

- Allow the emotion to exist for a moment without judgment and embrace the experience.

- When you're ready, begin taking long, slow, and deep breaths, imagining yourself in a safe place again. Open your eyes and take notes of your experience.

At the end of this chapter, you will find a prompt that will take you to your Workbook. You can use the empty pages provided to journal your experience with guided imagery.

Sensory Awareness

Sensory challenges can create a lot of anxiety and avoidance behaviors. Somatic practice can offer you a sensory break or help provide the sensory stimulation your brain and body crave. There are many different exercises that can help provide all kinds of sensory stimulation or relief. Here I'll focus on exercises for visual, audial, and tactile awareness.

Eye-Tracking

This exercise is great for providing visual sensory stimuli while calming the mind and body. It can also help increase your eyes' ability to focus and your depth perception as an added bonus. To practice eye-tracking:

- Choose any small object that you can pick up and hold with one hand.

- Sit or stand up straight, holding the object out directly in front of you.

- Without moving your head, follow the object with your eyes as you move it around.

- You can trace the object in different patterns and experiment with different speeds.

- Have fun with it, and continue for as long as necessary.

This exercise can help with too much or too little visual stimuli, as it pulls your focus to one object while keeping your eyes engaged. It works to balance and focus your eyes for a relaxing effect.

Sensory Bottles

For this somatic exercise, you will need an empty bottle and some rice or other dry food products like lentils or beans. Fill the bottle about a third of the way with the dry food product. You can decorate the bottle or leave it as is and keep it handy. This exercise aims to provide a natural form of audial stimulation without the need for any technology, but it doubles as visual stimulation if necessary. To use your sensory bottle:

- Find a quiet place to sit, stand, or lie down.
- Take a few deep breaths and close your eyes for a moment.
- Lift the bottle up and gently raise either end to move the contents from left to right.
- Allow your awareness to fully sink into the experience, listening to the sounds your sensory bottle provides.
- For added visual stimuli, you can open your eyes and focus your awareness on the bottle's contents moving gently.
- Enjoy the experience for as long as needed.

If you enjoy the visual aspect of this exercise, you can play around with the bottle's contents, adding glitter, beads, buttons, or whatever else may provide adequate visual stimuli.

Self-Holding

Tactile stimulation is a great way to provide comfort during a stressful time for autistic people who enjoy deep pressure. However, weighted blankets are costly and there may not always be someone around who can give you a big hug. This is where the self-holding somatic exercise can provide great relief and comfort. To practice self-holding:

- Sit or lie down in a comfortable place.
- Place one hand firmly on your forehead and the other on your chest.
- Apply gentle pressure to these areas as you hold your hands in place.

- Bring your awareness to the sensation of the hand on your forehead. Notice any emotions or thoughts that come up and allow them.

- After a few moments, slowly bring your awareness to the space beneath your other hand. Notice how it feels to provide pressure to this area.

- Now, bring your awareness to the space between both hands, scanning your neck and shoulders for any tension or discomfort.

- Take a few deep breaths as you hold and notice.

- Keep breathing deeply and move the hand on your chest down to your stomach.

- Hold both hands in place again, bringing your awareness to the sensations underneath the hand on your stomach.

- Take a few more deep breaths and gently release your hands.

- Notice how you feel.

You can add other tactile stimulation steps to this exercise, such as wrapping your arms around yourself and applying pressure with your hands in a self-hug or bringing your knees up to your chest and hugging them tightly for a moment.

Now that you have read through all 15 exercises, think about which ones stood out to you most or which ones make the most sense for your unique challenges as an autistic adult. I'll encourage you to go to your Workbook and choose 5 somatic exercises that you can do daily in a dedicated safe space.

Your daily somatic routine can be as simple as spending 10 minutes in bed every morning or evening doing your exercises. But if possible, I recommend creating a space in your home where you can retreat and find comfort.

Knowing that you have a special form of active outlet for emotions, stress, and tension can help you feel more resilient throughout the day and give you the confidence to face more challenges. These exercises are also at your disposal to bring you relief at any time.

Stimming is such an integral part of the autistic experience for many of us. Somatic practice can serve as a way to deepen, validate, and fulfill our stimming needs. However, even for those of us who don't feel the need to stim, these exercises naturally come with a variety of benefits for improved overall well-being.

A daily somatic practice provides a safe space to explore ourselves and understand our experiences. It can drastically increase our mind-body awareness, allowing us to recognize our needs and offer ourselves support in times of stress or discomfort. Once we know what our needs are, it's important to accommodate them. Meet me in the next chapter to find out how.

TOOL #2: SELF-ACCOMMODATIONS

Easy Changes To Make The World More Comfortable For You

"Remember, if you ever need a helping hand, you can find one at the end of each of your arms."

– Audrey Hepburn

I loved my job in the crystal store. Every morning, I would unlock the door to enter a room filled with beautiful specimens of all shapes, colors, and sizes. My brain quickly became an encyclopedia filled with names like Rhodocrosite, Snowflake Agate, and Tourmaline. The other employees, just as passionate as me, befriended me easily. And the salary was good.

But nothing made up for the growing sense of dread I began experiencing on my way to work. Nothing stopped the increasing exhaustion I would feel when I got home. No amount of passion, camaraderie, or determination made it possible for me to continue. After 8 successful months, I met with my employer and resigned.

I didn't understand exactly what went wrong until I looked back years later and recognized the problem.

Every morning, I would wake up early, put on makeup, and make the effort to dress myself in a neat and fashionable outfit. I would drive to work in the busy traffic. I would smile, stand up straight, and politely answer customers' questions all day long. I had a very good, high-functioning exterior. But it came at a price.

The dread building on my way to work and the tears of exhaustion on my way home were warning signs I didn't recognize then but do now. I was heading toward burnout. But not because there was anything wrong with my job, my employer, or me. Everything was perfect except for one thing – I didn't know I was autistic.

When the lights felt too bright, I stood and bore them. When the mandatory essential oil burner smell changed to something too strong, I didn't say anything. When the holiday season approached, and the number of customers tripled overnight, I did my best to keep up. I couldn't. Instead, burnout took over, and I left my job wishing I didn't have to.

The truth is, had I known what I do now, maybe I wouldn't have had to.

If I had recognized the signs of being overwhelmed sooner and made the accommodations that I desperately needed, then things would have been different. Thankfully, after years of learning to understand my needs and self-accommodate, all areas of my life have improved significantly.

Self-accommodation is when you take your comfort levels and needs into your own hands and actively make the changes that you can to improve your life. It's not about what employers are willing to offer or what general accommodations are available in your country because you might not always have a lot of control over that.

But there is a lot about your life that you can control. Even little things like lighting or what you wear add up. As your second tool, I'd like to discuss the many small but significant accommodations you can make to build a life conducive to autistic thriving.

WHY ACCOMMODATIONS MATTER

As we discussed in Chapter 3, the autistic mind is far more active, even at rest. This can make the world feel intense, creating a host of sensory problems, masking requirements, and more. Autistic people are also 85% more likely to have comorbid psychiatric conditions and over 50% more likely to suffer from sleep disorders. They are at a much higher risk for a variety of other health problems like autoimmune disease and epilepsy.[15]

Overall, keeping up with our daily lives and functioning as best as we can takes considerably more energy than it does for healthy neurotypical people. We can't afford to let our energy go to waste on small stressors.

Some struggles self-accommodating may help with include:

- Scratchy clothing
- Bright lighting
- Cleaning your house
- Maintaining a healthy routine
- General hygiene
- Socializing
- Sensory overwhelm
- Finances

Self-accommodating allows you to save as much energy as you can. It is an opportunity to identify little ways to offer yourself relief and ease in all areas of your life. It's a powerful way for you to support yourself through your challenges.

ACCOMMODATIONS TO CONSIDER

Releasing any shame around using the accommodations I'm going to suggest will help you move forward with your well-being at the forefront. Your needs should always come first, above the comfort of others or maintaining a certain image.

You didn't come here to learn how to fit in better; you came to find solutions for the problems you are facing. And because you are on the spectrum, those solutions will likely be different from those that work for most people.

Be open to self-accommodating in whichever way works for you above whichever way seems most acceptable.

Sound

Sound sensitivities are a very common problem amongst autistic people. It may be a sensitivity to the general noise of life, loud, unexpected sounds, or certain frequencies. This is why not all sound accommodations will work for everyone. You may need to try:

- Noise-canceling headphones: to cancel out large amounts of noise.
- Earplugs: to help cancel out unexpected loud sounds.
- White or brown noise: to improve focus and relaxation.
- Music: for relaxation and emotional processing.

Depending on your sensory requirements, you may have to try to reduce sounds or add them. You can also combine sound accommodations. For example, if you have noisy neighbors, you can wear noise-canceling headphones and play relaxing background music with added white noise to help mask background sounds.

Lighting And Colors

Color and lighting are powerful enough to impact anyone's mood.[16] But for autistic people, there are additional issues with light sensitivity that can cause significant distress and anxiety. Certain colors may also feel overstimulating, as well as too many colors or patterns. A plain environment may also feel too understimulating for some autistic people. What's important is that you influence your living space as much as possible to meet your needs. This can include:

- Dimmable light switches: These are an often affordable way to lower the intensity of lighting in your home.

- Mood lighting: Find alternative ways to light your home that create a more relaxed environment, such as string lights, lamps, or colored LED strips.

- Color palettes: Choose a color pallet for your home that feels calming and enjoyable.

- Patterns: Stick to patterns that help balance your stimulation needs, and when in doubt, avoid them for things that can't be easily changed.

- Sunglasses: Don't be afraid to wear sunglasses indoors if you have to. They are a quick way to cope with harsh lighting in environments you can't control.

Enduring bad lighting may be enough to cause sensory overload. You may not always have control of the lighting in your environment, but when you do, make any changes you can for immediate relief. And if you have to spend long periods of time somewhere you don't have control of the lighting, find ways to make provisions, like wearing sunglasses or asking for accommodations from people who are in control.

Tactile

Our bodies experience so many tactile sensations in a day, from the clothes we wear, the bedding we sleep under, the chores we have to do, like washing dishes, and even the foods we eat. Textures, textiles, and other tactile stimuli can influence how we feel and even cause significant distress if left unchanged. Some tactile self-accommodations you can make include:

- Clothing: Prioritizing comfortable fabrics over fashion and cutting out clothing tags.

- Bedding: Using a heavier duvet or adding weight with extra blankets and choosing textiles that feel comforting.

- Food: Nutrition should always be a priority, but where possible, it's okay to stick to foods that are both nutritious and of a texture you enjoy.

- Fidget toys: When you feel a lack of tactile stimulation, there are plenty of different types of fidget toys, or stim toys, available for different tactile needs. There are even toys made specifically for adults, like fidget cubes or hand rollers.

Tactile issues can be distracting at the best of times. Even a lack of tactile stimulation can leave you feeling dysregulated. Slowly weed out the clothing in your closet that makes you uncomfortable, try new bedding arrangements, and let go of any stigma you may have against fidget toys.

Social

Accommodations don't always have to mean physical changes or new sensory-friendly items. Sometimes self-accommodating means making choices that better meet your needs, such as changing how you socialize. This can include:

- Unmasking: Finding people, places, and activities that require less masking, if any.

- Location: Choosing places to socialize that are enjoyable for you.

- Boundaries: Setting boundaries around who you spend time with, allowing more time with people you feel good around and less time with people who drain you.

- Communication supports: Bringing pre-written topics you'd like to talk about or visual aids like pictures.

- Alternative communication methods: Opting to supplement conversation with texting, writing, or with the help of communication apps.

- Online friendships: Enjoying stress-free interactions in safe online spaces like the LearnWell Community.

Socializing is one of the most common areas of difficulty for autistic people. Many of us are also nonverbal or partially nonverbal, which makes communication far more challenging without accommodations. We'll discuss communication skills and tactics for autistic adults in Chapter 9, but for now, try some of these changes to enjoy social interactions more.

Digital

Technology is incredible. Most of us have smartphones or computers in our homes, and there are many ways that they can act as a self-accommodation tool. Apart from communication, entertainment, and music, many excellent apps have been developed to make our lives easier. Apps to consider include:

- Mental health apps: There are many mental health apps available, offering a safe space to journal, answer caring prompts, jot down progress, and find support. For example, an app I personally use is Finch, a virtual pet with a to-do list, mood checker, journal, and more.

- Finance tracking: Apps designed to help you track your spending may help you keep your finances under control, reducing the stress that comes with it. Apps like Fortune City make finance tracking fun while offering useful overviews of your spending habits.

- Organization apps: Some organizational apps available work to help you stick to a routine in a fun and motivating way. You can try Habitica, which is designed to gamify everyday tasks and routines.

There are apps for almost anything you can think of. Use the ones that work for you, no matter how silly they may seem, and try some new ones if you need help with something that an app can assist with.

Home

Maintaining a living space that feels comfortable and clean isn't always easy. For some of us, it's so difficult that our homes can get out of hand quickly. But there are many housekeeping self-accommodations that may help you stay on top of things, like:

- Organization: Organized chaos is better than chaos. A great way to manage clutter is to place similar items together in separate containers or baskets. This way, you will always know where something goes when cleaning, and it'll be easy to find again later.

- Cleaning: Choose cleaning products that are unscented if smells are an issue, wear gloves to avoid getting your hands wet, and break overwhelming tasks up into smaller tasks. And if you're struggling, give yourself permission to ask for help.

- Comfort zones: If you have to maintain a larger space than you are able to properly maintain, choose a smaller area within that space that you know you can maintain. Prioritize keeping that space clean and comfortable so you always have at least one place to retreat to that feels good.

How you keep your living space is very personal. Self-accommodating with your home should only include things that will make your living needs easier to meet, like asking for or hiring assistance, organizing things in a way that works for you, and simplifying difficult home maintenance tasks. It's not about making sure your home meets a societal standard, only aiming to meet your own standards.

Hygiene

Hygiene is another common area of difficulty for many autistic adults. It can be caused by many things, such as sensory issues, hygiene anxiety, executive dysfunction, and difficulty remembering or performing tasks. Some self-accommodations that may help with common hygiene-related issues include:

- Showering: Depending on the cause of your shower aversion, you could try changing your shower gels to something unscented, playing relaxing music in the bathroom or getting a phone stand to allow calming entertainment, and asking a friend, partner, or family member to stay close by and support you.

- Brushing teeth: To support your teeth brushing schedule, work to make it as enjoyable as possible by choosing a toothbrush with a softer bristle strength, choosing toothpaste with a more pleasant flavor, and playing music to help make it more fun.

- Grooming: Some easy grooming changes you can make include getting a low-maintenance haircut, opting for scentless deodorants, and minimizing your grooming routine.

Avoidance is a common problem when certain hygiene-related tasks trigger anxiety. But you can self-accommodate by making small changes that may make those tasks more enjoyable. You can also use a mental health or organizational app to help remind you and motivate you.

Needing to accommodate yourself, even for tasks that seem basic or simple, is nothing to be ashamed of. In the spirit of embracing your autistic traits, implementing accommodations should be your next step. Wear headphones and sunglasses out in public if you need to. Watch your favorite comedy shows in the bathroom while you shower. Organize your home in a way that works, even if other people disapprove.

Improving your life will come from honoring your needs and making the changes necessary to live it to the fullest.

If you're unsure of where to start, take your time. Make use of the somatic exercises you learned in Chapter 3 to help you identify your needs and go from there. You don't have to make a bunch of changes at once. Start with just one thing and keep going. Keep working to make your life more comfortable and save as much energy as you can. There is an exercise waiting for you in your Workbook that may help you along. Do this now if you're ready, and meet me back here.

It's important that you find ways to conserve your energy where possible because there are other things just as vital to autistic thriving. Life is all about balance. Fun and joy should be a priority, too. But it may be more of a necessity than you realize, so turn the page now and learn how to prioritize joy the autistic way.

TOOL #3: PRIORITIZING JOY THE AUTISTIC WAY

The Importance Of Special Interests And Hobbies And How To Make Time For Them

*"One benefit of an overfeeling heart:
the smallest things can fill me with joy."*

– Anouk Vitte

On the ride home from school, my mom asked me what color she should paint my dresser. We often painted it to match my room. "Red and yellow," I said, to which she laughed and replied, "Of course." Those were the colors of almost everything else in my Winnie The Pooh-themed room.

My duvet cover, pajamas, and posters were all Winnie The Pooh. Every birthday, I'd unwrap at least one present and see that silly yellow bear. I had every character from the show lined up on my figurine shelf. And, you guessed it, my favorite teddy matched too. I would even fall asleep every night listening to Winnie The Pooh audio stories on my red and yellow cassette tape player. I could go on, but I'll spare you.

Winnie The Pooh was my first obvious special interest. It wasn't just a normal childhood obsession. It brought me a level of joy and comfort that made the world feel safe.

Seeing something from the franchise while out in public would light me up. Listening to the adventures on tape would pacify my nighttime anxiety. And I can't begin to describe the overwhelming swell of emotions that would stir through me when I would sit and watch the latest Winnie The Pooh movie releases. Little else could impact me the way this interest did. That's what made it a special interest.

An autistic special interest is a hobby or interest that is enjoyed and expressed to the extreme. What makes a special interest unique to autistic people is the indescribable sense of joy that it can bring – autistic joy.

While being autistic does come with many challenges, there are definitely advantages. Autistic joy, if allowed to blossom, is one of the many gifts that can come with ASD. Having unique brains that experience the world so intensely gives us access to an intense level of joy neurotypical people may not understand. This joy may pulse through us in a surge of positive energy and, if expressed, can bubble out in a happy display of movements, stims, tears, and vocalizations.

THE IMPORTANCE OF AUTISTIC JOY

Joy is an important state of being for everyone. It's so important that it has been shown to improve immune function, decrease stress hormones, and even help you live longer.[17] Most people may express their joy in a way that is deemed socially acceptable. But because autistic joy is so intense, we may express ourselves in ways that attract attention, make us feel judged, and cause us to suppress it. This may contribute to the host of struggles we are prone to, like depression, anxiety, loneliness, and poor health.

Autistic joy isn't just something to wait around and hope that it happens. To thrive as an autistic adult, it is essential to actively pursue joy. It's not a want, it's a *need*. Embracing your autism and finding new ways to be authentic means embracing your autistic joy, no matter how over the top it may appear. Give yourself permission to just be who you really are and express your unfiltered, intense happiness when it comes up. Doing this can:

- Promote positive emotions, allowing them to come more regularly.

- Make life feel more meaningful and fulfilling.
- Cultivate an improved level of self-expression and empowerment.
- Help you feel more resilient to stress and adversity.
- Fuel your motivation to explore the world and pursue more joy.
- Enrich your life with a greater sense of well-being.

Tapping into autistic joy requires experiences that truly light you up. If you're struggling with mental health, this can feel far-fetched. But the more you understand yourself and your autistic traits, the more you will find resources for autistic joy. One of the most effective resources is a special interest or hobby.

SPECIAL INTERESTS: THE KEY TO THRIVING

The key to autistic joy and, therefore, thriving is indulging in special interests. This is tool #3. These can include an intense passion for a specific topic, item, or activity.

For example, a stereotypical special interest often depicted in autistic children is trains. You might hear of a little boy spending hours learning about trains, lining up his toy train replicas, and excessively talking about them. Another example may be a child obsessed with some obscure scientific topic or an adult with an extensive action-figure collection. But special interests can be anything, including things that are considered "normal" or "age-appropriate."

It's also possible to experience special interests at varying degrees. You might spend hours researching a topic without constructing your entire life around it, or you might collect everything related to a topic without doing much research at all. You might have the same special interest your entire life, or you might go all out very quickly on new special interests every couple of months. Autistic people experience special interests uniquely, and some might not find value in them at all.

However, where there is joy, there is value.

To whatever degree you experience special interests or engage in hobbies, I'd like you to focus on things, places, activities, topics, or even people that bring you joy. Don't worry about whether or not the interest is age-appropriate; just be true to it. If the interest speaks to your soul, stirs up a profound level of passion within you, or brings you joy and comfort, lean into it.

I'm going to give you some tips on making time for special interests and hobbies, but let me explain why special interests themselves are so vital to autistic thriving. Above the intense joy or comfort they produce, they often come with benefits essential to the autistic experience, including:

- Sensory regulation: Many special interests or hobbies include some form of sensory element that can regulate sensory needs.
- Enhanced focus and attention: The passion driving special interests can provoke an intense focus and deep concentration. This can lead to increased productivity,

problem-solving, and mastery of unique talents, knowledge, or skills.

- Improved self-expression: Engaging in special interests openly or enjoying creative special interests offers an outlet for self-expression that can help you express your thoughts, feelings, and opinions in unique and fulfilling ways.

- Confidence building: Success and progress in a special interest can provide feelings of competence, capability, and self-esteem, which are three essential elements of confidence.

- Social connection: Special interests provide opportunities for positive social interactions as they encourage a sense of community, create shared interests, and potentially require time with other like-minded people.

- Decreased anxiety and depression: Engaging in a special interest can act as a powerful coping mechanism, helping to relieve overwhelming emotions and promote relaxation in times of stress.

- A sense of identity and purpose: Special interests can help you define who you are, what you like, and what brings your life meaning. This can help you develop a healthy sense of identity and find a sense of belonging.

- A source of joy: Making time for activities that you are passionate about is a powerful way to experience more joy and embrace your expression of this emotion.

If you know what your special interest is or feel drawn to explore a new topic or activity, all that's left to do is make time.

MAKING TIME TO EXPLORE SPECIAL INTERESTS

Although I no longer wear Winnie The Pooh pajamas to bed, not all my current special interests are what you would consider "age-appropriate." While self-development is by far one of my most expressed and practiced special interests, I still lean on my other more childlike interests, like Barbie and My Little Pony. It may sound silly for an adult to watch programs or collect toys designed for children, but I like to think of it as a soothing way to comfort my inner child – a part of me that is very much alive and full of extraordinary joy.

As an autistic adult, sometimes you have to find creative ways to regulate yourself. And if that means enjoying a program, collecting a toy, or even wearing themed pajamas around the house that others might consider weird or childish, do it.

Your happiness is more important than trying to fit the norms of society. Special interests allow you to choose your own happiness and embrace who you are. If you feel like something's been missing lately or you haven't smiled in a while, it may be time to enjoy a special interest.

To enjoy your special interests more, you can:

- Schedule dedicated time for them: If possible, choose at least one day a week when you can actively engage in your special interest.

- Pursue related training or studies: Deepen your related knowledge and skillset with professional studies or training opportunities.

- Join clubs or groups: Most interests have online forums, in-person clubs, or communities of like-minded people you can engage with. If possible, join them.

- Start a project and set a goal: Start a project related to your special interest and set an achievable goal that you can aim towards to help motivate more time on your special interest.

- Incorporate them into your daily routine: Find ways to make your special interests a part of your daily routine. For example, watch programs, read books, stick up posters, listen to music, or keep a phone wallpaper related to your interest.

- Make space for them in your home: If possible, create a dedicated place in your home to enjoy your special interests.

- Share your passion: Find ways to talk about your passion with other people or share what you can, such as art, progress, or information. You can also share online in groups or forums related to your topic.

- Explore related career opportunities: Sometimes, excessive knowledge, experience, or talent with a certain special interest may be useful in a professional setting. If possible, explore career opportunities related to your interests.

- Keep a journal about them: Write down your experiences to help track your progress and remind you of the importance of special interests. To cultivate some joy right now, your Workbook has an exercise dedicated to your special interest. Take a moment to go there now and indulge in it.

As your third tool, try to include your special interest in your life as much as possible to create ample opportunities for autistic joy. Remember, enjoying special interests is not a matter of wasting time or indulging in desires. They are an important form of regulation for autistic people. They are the key to autistic thriving. So, if you're ready to thrive, take time today to enjoy your special interest in whatever way you can. Then, when you're ready, turn the page for the next tool at your disposal – journaling.

TOOL #4: JOURNAL ACTIVITIES THAT SPAN THE SPECTRUM

How To Make The Powerful Practice Of Journaling Work For You

"Suppressing the feelings only makes it harder to let them go. Expression is the opposite of depression."

– Edith Eger

Imagine having a best friend that could fit inside your pocket. Whenever you felt stressed, wanted to talk about an exciting new interest, or just needed to vent, they were there. You could take them out and immediately feel the relief of their presence. Keeping a journal is a lot like that.

A journal can be anything you want it to be. There are no rules to journaling. Almost any form of it can improve your life. That's why keeping a journal is tool #4. You can use it to better understand your thoughts and emotions, write down goals and ideas, or even express yourself through pictures and colors. A journal is there for you. There are so many ways to make this one simple practice something you can enjoy and feel motivated to do – and I will encourage that.

In this chapter, I'll show you why it's vital that you start journaling today. I'll also give you a heap of amazing journaling exercises you can try, including some that are very specific to common autistic needs. So, whether you've ever thought about journaling and didn't know where to start, have an active journaling practice already, or think journaling is not for you, keep reading.

WHY JOURNALING WORKS

There are extensive benefits to a regular journaling practice, and they don't stop at improved mental health. Journaling has been proven, time and time again, to significantly improve both emotional and physical health.[18] It has been shown to help:

- Manage anxiety and depression.

- Decrease stress levels.

Tool #4: Journal Activities That Span The Spectrum

- Improve your mood.
- Control symptoms.
- Feel more confident.
- Increase feelings of wellness.

The benefits you experience will coincide with the exercises you choose to use. However, you can also do different exercises depending on your needs for the day to experience a holistic positive impact from journaling. Depending on which exercises you do, journaling works exceptionally well for autistic adults because it:

- Promotes self-expression. Your journal is a safe and familiar space to express yourself in the comfort of your own home or whenever needed.
- Emotionally regulates. Journaling helps to process and regulate emotions by providing a structured outlet for self-reflection and expression.
- Improves self-awareness. A regular practice encourages introspection and self-awareness by offering a dedicated time to reflect on strengths and challenges and identify personal patterns, sensory or emotional triggers, and coping strategies.
- Offers additional communication skills. Writing in a journal can help you practice articulating your needs and emotions more effectively. It can also help you hone in on your ability to communicate through writing.

- Journaling improves coping with change. It offers a tool for processing change by documenting experiences and maintaining a sense of continuity and stability between major life events or transitions.

- Betters sensory processing. A journal allows you to safely explore sensory difficulties to better identify triggers and develop strategies for improved coping and prevention of sensory overload.

- Helps with goal setting and motivation. Among the many uses of a journal, you can use it to set goals and journal about your achievements to improve motivation and feel more in control.

- Increases physical health. Research reports that expressive writing is linked to improved immune function, pain reduction, and lowered risks for certain health conditions.[19]

Expressing yourself and processing your day-to-day emotions is not just another basic tool for stress relief. It is an essential practice that can help keep your emotional and physical wellness in balance. This is especially true if you struggle with feelings of isolation, social difficulties, or problems with emotional regulation – things that many of us on the spectrum do.

Now that you understand why journaling works let's jump into some exercises that you can add to your daily routine.

10 JOURNALING EXERCISES FOR ASD

Journaling is very flexible, like a somatic practice. It doesn't have to take long, and it's a simple, cost-effective practice that

Tool #4: Journal Activities That Span The Spectrum

produces big results. It also doesn't have to include any writing at all. You can express yourself through drawings, pictures, or verbal expression.

This tool is like a best friend in your pocket, ready and available whenever you need it. Try the exercises that sound the most impactful to you, and see which ones you can add to your daily routine for better overall health.

1. Daily Emotion Mapping

Emotion mapping is a journaling practice used by psychologists in various ways. It is a tool used to help people describe and understand how a certain event was experienced emotionally. Sometimes, family therapists use this exercise to map out each family member's emotional experience of a shared event to compare and understand differences.[20]

For this journaling exercise, I'd like you to use emotion mapping as a daily practice to map out the events and emotions that occurred throughout your day. You will use a wheel diagram split into the different emotions you fluctuated between. See an example of a filled-out emotion map in your Workbook. This exercise will also work well for a weekly emotion mapping practice.

Emotion mapping works well when combined with many visual elements, so I will encourage you to use colors, pictures, and easy emotion labels to help get the point across. Use this exercise to increase self-awareness and better understand your emotions. There are a few blank emotion maps in your Workbook. Use one now and follow along using the events of the last 24 hours.

Step 1: Prepare Your Journal

It is helpful to have a dedicated journal for emotion mapping so you can easily reflect on past events. In your Workbook, you will find a blank emotion map available to try this exercise right now. However, in the future, you can prepare a journal by drawing out blank emotion maps ready for use. You can also create the same template on your computer if you prefer digital journaling.

Step 2: Identify The Day's Emotions

With the emotion map ready in your Workbook or journal, reflect on the emotions you have experienced throughout the last day. Think about any events that occurred, both good and bad, and see if you can identify specific emotions you experienced during each event.

Step 3: Map Your Emotions

Across the blank emotion map, jot out the main emotions you experienced in the order in which they arose. You can also jot down a short summary of the event that created each emotion. For example, "Anger" → My dog chewed up my favorite pair of shoes; "Relief" → I almost missed my bus but didn't; "Joy" → Meeting a friend at the bookstore was nice.

Step 4: Identify Triggers And Sensations

Now that you have the events and emotions mapped out reflect on each emotion. See if you can remember any thoughts or sensations that triggered the emotion. For example, if you thought, "I can never wear my favorite shoes again!" after seeing your dog's mistake, that thought was likely the trigger for feeling angry. Next to each emotion in the chart, write down any triggers you can recognize.

Next, reflect on each emotion and see if you can remember any sensations that caused you to recognize which emotion you felt. For example, if your cheeks flushed hot, your heart began to pound, and your facial expression felt tense and unhappy, these are all sensations associated with anger. Write down any sensations you felt with each emotion in the chart.

Step 5: Reflect On The Experiences

Practice self-compassion as you reflect on your experiences. Reflect on how you responded to each emotion. Notice whether you expressed your emotion or suppressed it. Try not to judge yourself for your reactions; simply reflect on them and see if you can recognize any patterns that emerge.

2. Expressive Writing

As one of the most effective and well-researched journaling exercises, expressive writing is a form of cathartic release.[21] It is an exercise that encourages uncensored exploration of thoughts, emotions, and experiences. It's an excellent tool for self-discovery, self-expression, and overall personal growth.

You can use it to work through a major emotional challenge, past events, and daily emotions. All you need is a journal and a pen, a safe space to express yourself, and the courage to explore your thoughts and emotions.

Step 1: Set An Intention

If you are starting this exercise in the midst of strong emotion, don't waste any time and begin writing straight away. However, if you've dedicated time to explore a challenge or emotions, set an intention for the writing session. This can be anything from choosing a life event to explore, reflecting on a particular struggle in your life, or questioning a thought or belief you have.

Step 2: Start Writing And Flow

Start writing without worrying about grammar or spelling. Just let the words flow out onto the page. Allow yourself to write whatever comes to mind, no matter how unstructured or messy it seems.

Step 3: Keep It Continuous

If you reach a point where you feel stuck, just keep the words flowing out. For example, if you're stuck and don't know what to write, say so! Write out, "Oh no, I'm stuck. I don't know what to write," and just keep going. Let your stream of consciousness keep flowing.

Step 4: Explore Your Emotions

As you write, tap into any emotions you may feel. Explore them and write down any thoughts or sensations that come along with them. This is a safe space and time to fully release your emotions.

Step 5: Reflect On Your Writing

When you feel like the writing session is over, stop and take a moment to reflect on what you wrote. Read it back and notice any shifts in perspective or revelations you may experience. Think about how you can apply what you learn to future experiences or what you can do to move forward from the experience in an uplifting way.

3. Solution Brainstorming

This journaling exercise is designed to help you find solutions to a specific problem. It can help you make an informed and well-thought-out decision when you aren't sure how to handle a situation in the most productive way.

Step 1: Think About The Problem You're Facing

Take a moment to consider the problem you're facing. Consider why it's difficult to solve and all the various aspects related to it, including who's involved, what it's about, and more.

Step 2: Create A Solutions Diagram

You can use a normal journal for this, a bigger piece of paper, a whiteboard, or your computer. Just set up a blank space where you can map out a spider diagram. Draw a circle in the center of your page and write down the problem inside.

Draw lines out from the circle to spaces where you will write potential solutions to the problem. Write down as many solutions as you can.

Step 3: Rank Your Solutions

Jot down the pros and cons of each. Then, rank your solutions from best to worst. For example, if you have 5 solutions, the worst would be ranked #5, and the best would be ranked #1.

Step 4: Reflect On The Solutions

Reflect on the solutions, taking your time to review them fully. If you come up with more during this reflection process, write them down. You might see multiple solutions that can work or some that can be applied together.

Step 5: Apply What You Learn

When you've found a viable solution to your problem, apply it and see how it goes. Later, you can journal about the outcome for a reflective experience that will further improve your problem-solving skills.

4. Write And Release

Some thoughts or experiences may feel too painful to ever write down on paper. You may also fear that writing them down may leave you exposed to other people finding and reading your deepest struggles.

However, holding on to these thoughts and experiences can be harmful. That's why a write-and-release journal exercise is great: It allows you to let it all out and release it in a way that feels right.

Step 1: Find A Safe Space

It's important to find a private place where you can safely practice this exercise without being disturbed. If you're nervous, ask a friend to be nearby or try it with your therapist. Be gentle with yourself, and prepare for a cathartic release.

Step 2: Purge Your Thoughts And Emotions

Allow your thoughts to flood out onto paper, holding nothing back. This is an opportunity to truly dig deep and express the thoughts and feelings you may never want anyone else to know. You may have unresolved shame or feelings about someone, or you may have done things you regret. This is the time to free yourself of those things and prepare to let them go.

Step 3: Reflect On What You Wrote

Sit with the paper for a moment. Reflect on what you wrote and allow the emotions to surface without judgment. This exercise is all about releasing.

Step 4: Safely Release The Pages

When you're ready, imagine yourself releasing what you wrote down as you dispose of the paper. You can decide how you want to physically release the paper. Some good options include burning, shredding, or tearing up—whatever you can do safely and effectively to ensure satisfaction.

Step 5: Reflect On How You Feel

Now that the paper is gone and you've mentally worked on releasing what you wrote down reflect on how you feel. Notice any sensations in your body, any thoughts, and any behaviors you feel called to do. For example, you may feel lighter and mentally clear, or you may feel the need to rest. Honor how you feel, and take time to process the shift.

5. Gratitude Journaling

Gratitude journaling is one of the most uplifting exercises you can do daily for improved mental and physical wellness. It's simple and doesn't need to take more than 5 minutes in total. It's a great way to start your day or reflect on the good in your life for a better night's sleep.[22]

Step 1: Center Yourself

Take a moment to breathe deeply, centering yourself into the present moment. Close your eyes if you'd like to, focus on your breathing, and ground yourself gently.

Step 2: Reflect On 5-10 Things

Reflect on the things in your life for which you are grateful. Sometimes, it may feel hard to come up with something significant, but anything counts. Even if it's as simple as being grateful for the roof over your head, the small moments of success you experience, and someone in your life, just take a moment to let 5-10 things reveal themselves.

Step 3: Write Them Down And Notice

Write down the 5-10 things you are grateful for in this moment. Reflect on them and notice how you feel. Notice any shifts in perception and emotion. Spend a moment in this bubble of gratitude before continuing with your day or going to bed.

6. Emotional Identification

The purpose of emotional identification journaling is to better recognize and label various emotions as you experience them. This will help you understand the emotion and take the necessary steps to regulate it. It's best used when experiencing an intense emotion that you may be struggling to identify or process or to reflect on a past experience.

To help you with this exercise, there is an emotions chart in your Workbook depicting various emotions followed by an emotions wheel including all the complex variations of emotions. Use these as a visual aid to help you recognize emotions in others and yourself.

Step 1: Take A Moment To Notice

Pause for a moment as you notice how you feel. Take in any sensations, thoughts, and behaviors that arise, such as tightness in your shoulders, biting your nails, and thinking about an upcoming event. Don't judge how you feel. Just be curious and notice.

Step 2: Write Down What You Feel

Make notes of all the things you are feeling and thinking. You can list them separately under "Sensations," "Thoughts," and "Behaviors."

Step 3: Try To Label The Emotion

Do your best to connect the dots of how you feel and label the emotion. You may also be experiencing a combination of emotions. Use the chart in your Workbook if needed to help you identify the emotion accurately.

Step 4: Meet The Need

Once you know which emotion you are dealing with, try to meet the need of that emotion. You can do this by releasing the emotion with somatic practice, journaling about the emotion, or taking steps to resolve it.

7. Prompts For Self-Reflection

A great way to enter a state of self-reflection and increase self-awareness is to use journal prompts. Journal prompts offer a way to jump into journaling easily without needing to think about what to write. Simply choose a few prompts from this list and answer them in your journal.

Your Workbook provides space to complete each of these prompts when you're ready. However, many journal prompts are useful to do regularly. In this case, simply prepare your journal by writing down prompts in advance and leaving space to answer them.

Journal Promps To Try

- If I had no financial limitations, what project or activity would I start right now?

- What was one thing that happened to me today that made my day better?

- If I could wish for one thing right now, what would it be?

- What is one thing that I could do today to improve my life?
- Find a picture you like, and write a short story inspired by it. Reflect on it.
- If my younger self could be here right now, how old would she be, and what would I say to her?
- Reflect on your daily routine and write down any improvements you could make.
- Choose a special interest or hobby and write down everything you love about it.
- Describe a sensory experience from your day. Write down whether it was enjoyable or not, what sensations you felt, and how you responded to it.
- Choose 3 words to describe yourself today. Write them down and ask yourself whether they're accurate, helpful, or hurtful.

8. Scoring

This is an easy addition to any journaling exercise and can form part of your general journaling preparation. It's a quick way to keep score of certain conditions that can impact your mood and productivity, such as anxiety, depression, stress, or pain. Keeping track can help you acknowledge how you feel and reflect back on your progress.

To include scoring in your routine, simply score your condition on a scale of 1-10, with 1 being barely present and 10 representing an overwhelming impact. For example, if you have very high anxiety to the point of experiencing a panic attack, you can score your anxiety a 10 for the day.

9. Creative Expression

Journaling doesn't have to include writing. The point of journaling is to express yourself, work through struggles, and note triumphs. However, this can be done through creative expression journaling.

To enjoy creative expression journaling, you can use any form of creative medium to express your emotions, thoughts, and experiences. Some creative expression ideas include:

- Creating a collage.
- Drawing about an experience.
- Painting your mood.
- Coloring in a picture from an adult coloring book.
- Creating a visual representation of an emotion.
- Preserving memories in a scrapbook.
- Creating a song or making music about an experience.
- Collecting small mementos from positive experiences in a jar or shoebox.

You can express yourself and process emotions in any creative way that feels good to you. What's important is that you reflect on your art or collected items to process what they mean to you.

10. Sensory Or Symptom Diary

Some forms of journaling are purely practical, helping you to identify patterns in your lifestyle that may be harmful to you. A sensory or symptom diary is a great way to keep track of experiences that trigger sensory overload or chronic illness symptoms.

Choose a separate diary for this purpose. You can pick a time of day to journal your experiences, or you can keep your diary with you to jot them down straight away. Ensure you include as much detail as possible, including the emotions that came with the experience.

Diarizing your sensory experiences or symptoms can help you recognize patterns in your lifestyle, thoughts, and behaviors that may be contributing to your discomfort. Reflect back on what you've diarized regularly to find new ways to cope.

A journaling practice doesn't need to take up a lot of time. It can take as little as 5 minutes in your daily schedule to complete an exercise. It's something that you should mold to meet your needs, finding ways to make it enjoyable, relieving, and more impactful for you.

Journaling is a powerful tool that can make a tremendous difference both physically and mentally in times of stress. Let your journal become a friend in your pocket that you visit regularly to express yourself, reflect, and learn.

I hope that you enjoyed the exercises in this chapter and are feeling more at ease within yourself. Turn the page now and meet me in Chapter 7, where we will delve into the often frustrating issue of executive dysfunction and find new solutions to the problem.

TOOL #5:
THE GAME OF
EXECUTIVE DYSFUNCTION

Using Play And Rewards For Improved Executive Functioning

"Play keeps us vital and alive. It gives us an enthusiasm for life that is irreplaceable."

– Lucia Cappachione

You see the washing that needs to be folded lying in a growing pile on the floor. There's a funny smell starting to float out of the kitchen. Your pantry is in desperate need of restocking. The list of things you need to get done gets longer. You desperately *want* to take action. But there's something holding you back – executive dysfunction.

Executive dysfunction is a heavy burden that weighs on your body, making the smallest tasks feel like mountains. It's the cloud in your mind when you trip over your words or forget what you were doing so often it becomes crippling. It's the feeling of overwhelm as one missed task quickly overflows into an ocean of unwashed dishes, laundry piles, and missed work deadlines.

To properly define it, you must understand what executive *functioning* is and why it is often the crux of getting things done.

Executive functioning is our brain's ability to help us monitor, prioritize, start, and finish tasks. But these tasks can span any area of our lives, from maintaining a job to having a structured conversation. There are 8 areas of normal executive functioning:

- Working Memory: The ability to remember details, instructions, and thoughts and accurately convey them to others.

- Emotional Control: Managing emotions to avoid outbursts and arguments.

- Inhibition: Knowing when to stop a behavior at the appropriate times and controlling impulsions.

- Initiation: Starting tasks comfortably and at the appropriate times.

- Shifting: Switching between tasks without an issue and coping well with sudden change.

- Planning: Keeping track of current and future tasks and planning for them effectively.

- Organizing: Keeping material items in order and maintaining an organized space.

- Self-monitoring: Understanding and being able to regulate our own behavior.

Successful executive functioning allows a person to manage their lives without becoming negatively affected by the effort. However, executive dysfunction is when the same effort applied to maintain your life comes at a cost.

You may keep up with tasks but feel drained, depressed, or anxious. Or, you may struggle to keep up with tasks in order to maintain mental health. It's something that can impact anyone, but is a very common symptom of ASD and other neurodivergence.

Executive dysfunction is also on a spectrum. It can occur to any degree and includes a variety of executive functioning struggles. For example, you may struggle to maintain a clean house but comfortably keep up with a full-time job. You may have no problem initiating tasks but struggle to follow through. You may manage your environment successfully without being able to get through a conversation concisely. You may even believe that executive dysfunction is not an issue for you, even though keeping

Tool #5: The Game Of Executive Dysfunction

your life together leaves you anxious and exhausted at the end of each day. The most important thing about executive dysfunction is that you are aware of it.

You'll need something before you continue. It's the only way to manage your executive functioning issues and see lasting change. You'll need to summon a sense of compassion for yourself.

Recognize that you are not to blame for executive dysfunction. It's a real problem that spurs from developmental issues in the brain. For example, people with another closely linked neurodivergence, ADHD, have been shown to develop over 30% slower in the regions of the brain responsible for executive functioning.[23]

Neurodivergence is a difference in the physical make-up of your brain. It's not something you can just suddenly decide not to have. It will take understanding, patience, and time to figure out how to navigate executive dysfunction in a way that works best for you. However, let this chapter help speed up the process.

There are tried and tested models for coping with executive dysfunction and many creative ways to make those models work for you. You're going to need to work *with* the wiring of your brain, finding ways to encourage positive executive functioning development. Keep reading, and let's unravel this frustrating problem with tool #5: fun and rewarding solutions to executive dysfunction.

SPOON THEORY: THE TRADITIONAL APPROACH

Spoon Theory started as a metaphor created by Christine Miserando while she was having dinner with her friend. She suffered from Lupis and used the metaphor to explain her experience of having limited energy each day to complete tasks. If she did too much, her "spoons" would run out, and she would have to deal with the consequences of a flare-up in symptoms.

However, it has now blossomed into a useful way to better organize the limited energy you may have daily due to chronic illness, mental health problems, or neurodivergence. It's a great way to help manage executive dysfunction, as low energy is a common trigger.

The traditional way to use spoon theory involves choosing a set number of "spoons" to represent your daily energy budget. You then organize daily tasks listed under the amount of spoons they require. As you plan your day, you can decide which tasks are a priority and delegate your spoons accordingly. A daily spoons chart may look like this:

- Get out of bed
- Brush teeth
- Get dressed
- Take meds
- Watch tv

- Read a book
- Text people
- Pick up food
- Use computer
- Style hair

- Take a shower
- Study
- Cook a meal
- Room cleaning
- Shopping

- Work / school
- Socialize
- Run errands
- Exercise
- Home cleaning

Tool #5: The Game Of Executive Dysfunction

Using spoon theory to manage your energy can help you avoid feeling burnt out, having meltdowns, or slipping into shutdown. It's a great way to remind yourself that your energy is limited. Everyone's energy is. But remember, ASD brains process information much faster than neurotypical brains, so you naturally use more energy at rest. This is where spoon theory helps.

While the traditional spoon theory approach may require you to drastically simplify your life, I'm not here to suggest that. There's an adjustment you can make to maximize your daily energy and enjoy your life without hitting a wall. The only thing you need to know is that not all activities take energy.

I'd like you to try using spoon theory to help manage your energy with the addition of tasks that *replenish* spoons. So, if you start your day with 12 spoons and they're running out fast, take time to do something that can give you a few more to work with. Examples of activities that may give you spoons include:

- Rest and sleep
- Listening to music
- Engaging in a special interest
- Practicing mindfulness
- Spending time in nature
- Self-care practices
- Gentle exercise like yoga or walking

The activities that replenish your energy will be unique to you. You will know when something gives spoons back based on how you feel afterward. If you feel more rejuvenated and energized, then you can list it under your activities that replenish spoons. This list is there to help remind you of the things you can do when you're feeling low on energy. Allow yourself a break from daily tasks to enjoy an activity from this list when needed. Your new spoons chart might look like this:

- Get out of bed
- Brush teeth
- Get dressed
- Take meds
- Watch tv

- Read a book
- Text people
- Pick up food
- Use computer
- Style hair

- Take a shower
- Study
- Cook a meal
- Room cleaning
- Shopping

- Work / school
- Socialize
- Run errands
- Exercise
- Home cleaning

- Rest and sleep
- Listening to music

- Engaging in a special interest
- Practicing mindfulness

- Spending time in nature
- Self-care practices

- Gentle exercise like yoga or walking

I'll encourage you to either create and print out your own chart or use the chart we've created for you in your Workbook. Use it as a reference point for planning your day according to your energy levels. For example, if you wake up feeling drained, you may be having a "low spoon" day. Delegate your energy according to energy levels, and be sure to include more replenishing activities on "low spoon" days.

Spoon theory is there to help you manage and plan your energy around daily tasks. It gives each task a set amount of spoons required to complete it. However, what if you could lower the energy cost of certain tasks and free up energy while getting things done?

Well, there are ways to make mundane tasks easier without having to avoid them. I'm talking about a new spin on things that can make boring tasks fun, difficult tasks more rewarding, and energy-heavy tasks feel lighter.

A NEW SPIN ON THINGS: 5 FUN WAYS TO IMPROVE EXECUTIVE FUNCTIONING

If a mountain appears too big to climb, it'll be difficult to feel motivated to climb it. But if you could break the mountain up into small hills decorated with flowers, the same distance suddenly becomes achievable. Executive dysfunction is often not about an inability to complete tasks because they are overwhelming but rather because they appear overwhelming. There are 5 things you can do to make your mountains climbable:

- Break the mountain up into hills.
- Make climbing the mountain fun.
- Combine climbing with energizing activities.
- Plan your climb so it feels more achievable.
- Use tools to make climbing easier.

There are so many ways to make big, overwhelming tasks more doable, such as working with your brain to help bypass executive dysfunction. Let's go into more detail for each of the 5 methods and learn how you can apply them to your life.

Break The Mountain Up Into Hills: Rewarding Small Wins

When you have one big task to get done, not only does it feel more daunting, but you also get the reward of finishing the task once. You have to put a big amount of effort in before you can feel good about it, setting you up for overwhelm and shame if you fail.

However, if you break your big tasks up into smaller tasks, you can feel good every time you get a smaller task done. You break the task into achievable steps, setting yourself up for more success. To break a big task up, consider the steps required to complete it.

For example, if you need to clean your kitchen, the steps may include:

- Doing the dishes
- Mopping the floor

- Cleaning the counters
- Packing away groceries
- Washing dish towels

It's a lot to do all at once, so consider each step a separate task to reduce the mental load. Then, think about how you can make completing tasks more rewarding. For example, you can complete one replenishing activity after each smaller task, spread the tasks out across the entire day, or even reward yourself with small gifts like your favorite snack, points on a chart, or money in a jar. The idea is that you allow yourself to feel good about accomplishing a task, no matter how small.

The more you learn to notice and reward your effort, the more motivated you will feel to do more. Rather than being hard on yourself for taking a whole day to clean your kitchen, acknowledge that you found a way to do something difficult.

Make Climbing The Mountain Fun: Gamifying Your Tasks

There is a fun way to make mundane tasks more rewarding and enjoyable. It's called gamifying your tasks. This is when you add elements of play and games to your tasks to trick your brain into believing you're having fun and not completing a boring necessity. Some great examples of gamified tasks include:

- Standing on one leg while brushing your teeth: Doing this shifts your focus from the potential discomfort of brushing to the game of trying to stay balanced.

- Introducing constraints like time to a task: Sometimes, making a boring task more challenging can help summon more motivation to do it.

- Pretending to be a character completing the task: Letting your imagination play a role in your tasks can help make them more fun. For example, imagine that you are an explorer on the hunt for treasure to get yourself to go for a hike.

- Adding narrative storytelling elements to a task: Another way to engage your imagination and make tasks more fun is to add storytelling elements like a backstory and a plot to a task. For example, if you are a mom needing to pack away your child's toys, say to yourself, "The autistic mom sighs as she picks up toy after toy."

- Visual task tracking: You can activate your brain's reward centers more easily by having a visual presentation of your task progress. For example, you can fill a clear glass jar with marbles, where 1 marble equals 1 task. Then, when the jar is full, you can set up a big reward, like eating out or doing something you don't normally get to do.

The idea of gamifying your tasks is to break free from taking them too seriously. Often, the emotional pressure behind completing a task strips away your motivation and ability to do it. Try to incorporate more fun and creative spins on difficult tasks to help you release the intensity and seriousness of life. Don't worry about being a little silly sometimes; life is allowed to be fun.

Combine Climbing With Energizing Activities: Pairing High Spoon Tasks With Activities

There's nothing stopping you from using replenishing activities to help lighten the load of high-spoon tasks. If a task requires a certain number of spoons that exceeds your energy budget, you can pair it with a replenishing activity to help give you enough energy to complete it. For example, you might:

- Listen to music while cleaning the house or going shopping.

- Use car rides to have a karaoke session with yourself or your family.

- Watch your favorite TV program while showering or bathing.

- Reply to emails from your phone while having a lie down on the couch.

- Find ways to incorporate your special interest into tasks if possible.

- Plan social meetups in a natural environment, like the park, instead of a restaurant.

- Practice mindfulness while eating, breathing, and bringing your awareness to every bite.

If there are things that make difficult tasks easier, use them. Sometimes, a distraction is the best way to get through a boring task without needing to think about it. Executive dysfunction is rooted in the brain, so thinking about a task too much can be the very thing that stops us from doing it. Take action before you get a chance to think, and distract your mind with something you enjoy.

Plan Your Climb So It Feels More Achievable: Using Charts And Planners

Without a structured plan to help you get tasks done, you leave it all up to your brain in the spur of the moment. Charts and planners are a highly effective way to feel more organized and motivated. They help you do all the thinking when you have the energy so that the "doing" part of the task becomes easier. Between memory issues and planning problems, charts and planners go a long way to improve multiple executive functioning struggles.

But there are fun ways to organize tasks. Planners can be as neat and clean-cut as you like them, but they can also be colorful and fun. Charts don't have to be boring. They can be exciting and silly. If the chart is enjoyable for you to look at and engage with, you're more likely to actually use it. Some creative ideas you can use to make task organization more accessible include:

- Using an interactive diagram to mark progress. For example, a picture of a battery that you can color in to mark your energy levels throughout the day.

- A themed planner. For example, if you love boats, you can find a boat-themed planner to use to increase the appeal of using it.

- Gamify your progress tracker. For example, make a to-do list and add experience points to each task. Draw a progress bar that fills up with each task completed. When you fill a bar, you can "level up" and update your "character level."

Tool #5: The Game Of Executive Dysfunction

- Create a vision board. Vision boards are a creative way to stay focused on a particular outcome or life goal. You can fill it with pictures, affirmations, and anything else that makes you feel inspired to continue working towards your goal.

- Adventure map planner. Rather than a structured planner, you can create a treasure map with points that get you from the start to the treasure. Make each point an important task to reach a particular goal. As you complete a task, connect the dots as if you're walking the map.

- Organize a weekly quest board. If to-do lists feel outdated, try making a weekly Quest Board. This is where your tasks are labeled as quests, and you can include a reward for completing a quest.

- Use a reward chart. Reward charts are a great way to visually represent your progress and feel rewarded after each task. You can use a graph labeled something like "Tasks Completed" and stick a sticker on the chart whenever you complete a task. You can also choose to reward yourself in some way for every certain number of stickers you accumulate. There is a rewards chart in your Workbook you can use to test out this method and see if it works for you.

Planning and organizing tasks can be something you look forward to. There is no rule book for being an adult. Find ways to plan and organize your tasks, goals, and events that work for you, no matter how silly they may seem. If it adds joy and ease to an otherwise mundane or stressful area of your life, give yourself permission to use it.

Use Tools To Make Climbing Easier: Apps For Executive Function Support

You don't need to do everything yourself. If there is an app that can help take care of something for you, why not save yourself energy? Just like using a walking stick can make climbing a mountain easier, even if you can walk fine without it, there are apps that can support your executive functioning skills. Some free apps that can help with executive dysfunction include:

Pomodoro Timer

This is an app that allows you to manage your time using the Pomodoro timer method. This method allows you to focus on one task for 25 minutes at a time with 5-minute breaks in between. It helps you get into a good rhythm and stay energized while being productive.

Goblin Tools: Magic ToDo

This is an online app that uses AI to help you divide big tasks into smaller ones. You can simply type in a big task such as "Clean the kitchen," and with one click of a button, AI will divide it into a list of smaller tasks that you can then organize and check off.

Gratitude: Self-Care Journal

This app is an all-in-one self-care journal that includes prompts, affirmations, and many other self-care exercises. It can help you manage your emotions and build more self-awareness.

Quizlet

Quizlet is a great app for improving working memory. It allows you to create easy flashcards of things you'd like to remember, helping you learn something new without needing to memorize extensive notes.

More Apps For Planning And Organizing

There are many apps that are simply interfaces you can use for all your general organization and planning needs. However, there are also some that are more specific, such as cooking and cleaning apps. Here are a variety of planning and organization apps worth trying:

- Sweepy: Cleaning app for tracking chores, creating a cleaning schedule, and even competing with others on the app for extra cleaning motivation.

- Samsung Food: Meal planning app for Android and iOS devices with recipes and a weekly planner for meals.

- To-Do List Schedule Planner: An app with multiple organization and planning tools, including various to-do lists, reminders, and a calendar.

Choose whichever apps appeal to you and try using one until you notice the difference it makes.

Between apps and all the other ways that you can improve your executive functioning, it may take some time to find what works for you. What's important is that you recognize how executive dysfunction may impact your life and take steps to support yourself more.

Pressure is the bane of executive functioning. Remember to be compassionate with yourself and know that getting things done does not reflect your worth. Have patience with your brain and try to work with it as much as possible by finding new ways to feel motivated and energized.

Distraction can also play a role in executive dysfunction, so become aware if this is a problem for you and work to reduce it. Instead of just working to improve your executive functioning, take steps to remove any obstacles making it harder.

For example, if your phone is something that can grab your attention easily while you're trying to complete a task, put it out of sight or reach. If being indoors is too comfortable, take your tasks outside if you can. Try to counteract your tendency to get distracted to reduce the risk of becoming overwhelmed as tasks pile up.

As an adult, you are likely responsible for yourself or have much more control over what you do with your life. This responsibility can come with a lot of weight to carry, but I'll encourage you now to fully embrace it.

Your lifestyle is also not the only thing I'd like you to take more control over, but your place in the world as well. If you're ready to start feeling more confident in life through progressive self-advocacy in conversations and relationships, meet me in Chapter 8.

TOOL #6: SIMPLE STEPS TO SELF-ADVOCACY

How To Find Your Stronghold In Conversations And Relationships

"You demonstrate love by giving it unconditionally to yourself. And as you do, you attract others into your life who are able to love you without conditions."

– Paul Ferrini

His words sang over me like a melody of sweetness. He wasn't capable of lying in my eyes. He said boundaries kept people believing that they were separate as if it were a bad thing. I felt wanted and taken care of—something I'd always longed for. But as the years went by, my mental health withered more and more.

It wasn't long before I couldn't tell where he ended, and I began. His thoughts consumed my mind, my actions were things he encouraged, and my moral compass was broken in two. I had little control over my life and felt switched off from who I was beneath the facade of cool girlfriend who was always up for anything. I went along with whatever he told me was okay, not knowing that once the relationship ended, I would be filled with shame and regret.

Broken and in therapy, it took years to recover my sense of identity and start facing the trauma of being in a relationship with a narcissistic man. "Sociopath" is what my therapist called him. Under her professional guidance, I was quickly shocked into the realization that I was not only miserable around this person but in danger.

I was in danger of experiencing worsening abuse and witnessing more of his traumatic drug-induced behavior. The shock ran through me as I realized that the words I trusted so fully were interlaced with the most intricate lies and manipulation.

I've always blamed myself for believing and holding such a deep trust for someone who was taking advantage of me, but the truth is autistic people are up to 80% more likely to experience exploitation of some kind.[24] It's also a very powerful reason why so many of us suffer from mental illness and increased suicidality.[25]

Studies have also shown that:

- Autistic people are up to 75% more likely to experience bullying.[26]
- 9 out of 10 autistic women have experienced sexual violence.[27]
- 84% of autistic people have suffered multiple forms of victimization.[28]

These statistics are the reality of what being autistic is often like in the world we live in. It is a harsh reality that we absolutely must address and be aware of for our own safety. There are also many factors that contribute to these statistics. As autistic people, we may struggle to differentiate truth from lies.[29] We may miss vital communication cues that signal someone's true intentions. We may struggle with isolation and accept friendship from people who seek to exploit us. And we may not have the skills to stand up for ourselves safely and effectively.

But I don't want these statistics to drive you into mistrust and fear. I want to help you build the skills to self-advocate when necessary so you can navigate the world with confidence. Self-advocacy is when you can notice that someone is mistreating you or overlooking your needs and can stand up for yourself in a safe and effective way.

Remember, it's not your fault that you are at risk, but there is a lot you can do to protect yourself. Being autistic doesn't make you weak; it makes you vulnerable. Vulnerability is only a negative trait when you're surrounded by people who wish to take advantage of you or hurt you. But around the right people, vulnerability can form a bridge of connection that lasts a lifetime.

In this chapter, we'll explore self-advocacy and discuss tool #6: an effective strategy for self-advocating in everyday social situations. A self-advocacy strategy is the armor that can protect you from being manipulated, exploited, and bullied. You don't have to be a victim. You deserve to live your life and safely enjoy the company of trustworthy, like-minded people. Let's dive into when you might need to self-advocate and then how.

WHEN TO SELF-ADVOCATE

Any place or time where you need to interact with other people is a time to keep your self-advocacy strategy near. There will be times when you need to self-advocate in a professional setting, like a business meeting or doctor's visit, but there will be times when you might need to self-advocate around family, too. Let's break down the different social scenarios that may require you to self-advocate. You should be prepared to self-advocate:

During A Doctors Visit

Struggling to articulate symptoms and express your needs effectively around doctors can impact the quality of treatment you receive. Many general practitioners are also not specialized in the comorbidities that autistic people are at risk for, making accurate diagnosis more difficult. It often takes a doctor with a personal understanding of autism to get the help that you need. Some doctors may even hold misconceptions about autism, leading to mistreatment or neglect.

In Therapy

Unless a therapist specializes in adult autism, you may experience a lower quality level of treatment. Misinformed therapists may also prescribe medications and treatment options that lead to further problems. It's important to be able to tell whether a therapist is knowledgeable enough to offer you the right support. Unfortunately, therapy is also not free from people looking to exploit vulnerable patients.

At Work

If your employer, employees, or coworkers know that you are on the spectrum, they may hold their own prejudice about autistic people, leaving you at risk of bullying or exploitation. If they are unaware, your potential differences in behavior and communication may also put you at risk.

However, other problems among employers, employees, and coworkers who understand autism may include unintentional infantilization. This is when someone treats you like a child in an unintentionally condescending way.

Within Friendships

Friendships carry many potential risks for autistic people. It's important to be able to discern true friends from exploitative friends. Bad friends may engage in peer pressure, bullying, abuse, and neglect. It may also be difficult to know someone's intentions for friendship. If isolation is an issue for you, it's even more important to discern someone's intentions to avoid accepting mistreatment in exchange for social engagement.

Among Family

Family should always have your best intentions at heart. But even the most well-meaning family member may overstep your boundaries. They may talk for you, make decisions for you, or do things without your permission.

Even if you are nonverbal, there are ways to communicate your needs. Even if you need assistance from family, you should still play a vital role in decisions made for you. And no matter what, your personal boundaries should always be respected. For example, nobody should force you to hug them if you don't want to, even if they're family.

In Romantic Relationships

Romantic relationships are another high-risk relationship where self-advocacy is of the utmost importance. With the added potential for intimacy, there is an added level of exploitation risk. Emotions are also often far more involved and intense within romantic relationships, and love for someone can influence what you are willing to do for them.

Around Strangers

There are many scenarios where you may have to interact with strangers or people you don't know well. For example, speaking to cashiers, waiters, bus drivers, police officers, or any other public service provider. You may also interact with strangers at events or in public spaces like the park. It's important to be prepared to self-advocate in these scenarios because you may not know what the person is capable of.

YOUR SELF-ADVOCACY STRATEGY

Having a strategy in place to help you self-advocate can help you reduce your risk of being victimized, but it can also improve your self-confidence. There's no one you should trust more than yourself. Self-advocacy places you at the center of your world so that you're less likely to be swept up by somebody else. Having a strategy will allow you to feel more secure in social settings as you'll have a practiced routine of steps you can take if you're unsure of somebody.

However, before we discuss this in more detail, let's discuss some of the warning signs of abuse or bad intentions. Your strategy will need to account for these signs.

Warning Signs You Need To Self-Advocate

There are many signs that you can look out for that may indicate someone is taking advantage of you, has bad intentions, or is not respecting your boundaries. They can also simply be signs that someone is not a good person to build a relationship with. All of these signs require self-advocacy to ensure that your relationships are healthy. They include:

- Feeling extreme discomfort around someone specific.
- Friendliness that seems extreme or unwarranted.
- Aggressive behavior directed at you or someone else.
- Negative comments about you or someone you love.
- Aggression toward animals or disregard for their wellbeing.

- Touching you without consent.
- Controlling behavior, like telling you what to wear, think, or do.
- Threatening negative consequences for not complying with their rules.
- Exhibiting jealousy and possessiveness when you interact with others.
- Trying to get too close to you too quickly.
- Having unrealistic expectations of you.
- Unpredictable behavior, such as mood swings or actions that seem unexpected.
- Offering you something in return for affection or favors.
- Pressuring you into doing things you're not comfortable with.
- Calling you "too sensitive" or telling you that you're "overreacting."
- Forced interactions without your consent, such as hugging or other intimate touching.
- Doing things to embarrass you in front of other people.
- Calling you names or swearing at you.
- Denying your story of events, also known as "gaslighting."
- Ignoring requests to stop unwanted behavior or crossing other boundaries.

If you're in doubt about someone's behavior, always trust how you feel around them first. If you feel drained, unhappy, or anxious around a particular person, pay attention and follow the strategy we'll cover next. You can also ask someone you trust to confirm how you feel about someone or talk to a therapist.

The ABCD Self-Advocacy Strategy

Keep these signs in mind, and know that it only takes 1 sign for you to self-advocate. You don't need to wait until you're sure, either. You can take steps to feel safer straight away, starting with the strategy I've created for effective self-advocacy in any situation. It's called the ABCD strategy for self-advocacy, and it stands for:

A - Ask questions

B - Build Boundaries

C - Communicate

D - Do Something

Let's discuss how you can apply each of the steps in more detail. You will apply them differently in different situations, so it's important that you take this all in before trying the strategy. Your safety is the most important thing when self-advocating. Be sure to study this strategy and find the confidence to apply it effectively in the situations you may need it for.

Step 1: Ask Questions

The first and most important step in the ABCD strategy is to ask questions. But this doesn't mean asking questions out loud. It means asking yourself questions about your surroundings, other people, and behavior. It's all about noticing what is happening around you and asking yourself, "Is this normal?" Asking questions about these things is also known as practicing discernment.

You might also ask yourself:

- How do I feel about this?
- Do their emotions match the situation?
- Was that behavior warranted?
- Did I consent to that?
- Am I safe to be alone with this person?
- Would I have done that if they hadn't told me to?
- Can I be myself around this person?
- Can I notice any of the warning signs in this situation?

Step 2: Build Boundaries

Once you've questioned the situation at hand, the next step is to ensure that your boundaries are in place. Whether you notice signs or not, boundaries are important to withhold. You should even maintain boundaries with family, friends, and romantic relationships. All healthy relationships have boundaries to keep the people within them feeling respected and safe.

However, boundaries have layers. They are not always the same for each person. You will have your core boundaries that keep you feeling comfortable around everyone, including people you are intimate with. However, you should also have boundaries that you set around strangers or unsafe people. Your core boundaries should include:

- Your comfort levels regarding touch and personal space.
- How you allow people to speak to and treat you.
- The level of trust you have with people.
- Your limits regarding what you will do for others.
- The things you are comfortable sharing with others.

Other boundaries you should consider include:

- How much time you're willing to give someone.
- How often you will tolerate arguments or negative interactions.
- Who you are willing to spend time around.
- Your financial limits regarding social activities.
- Your intimacy boundaries within romantic relationships.

The more clear you can get about your boundaries, the easier it is to enforce them. When you are secure in your boundaries you can confidently stand your ground when someone tries to cross them. That's why it's important to take a moment now and write down your 5 most important boundaries. These are boundaries that must be upheld and protected at all costs, no matter who you're around. Please find the space provided in your Workbook and list your 5 core boundaries. Use the examples above to help you if needed.

Step 3: Communicate

If you feel that someone has crossed a boundary or that they are about to, you have an opportunity to communicate your discomfort. You can do this in multiple ways, even without saying a word. To self-advocate for a boundary, you can:

- If possible, use your words to clearly state your boundary. For example, "I don't like to be touched. Please don't touch me."

- Use your hands to signal disapproval, such as holding your hands up between you and someone trying to hug you.

- Use your body language to express disapproval. For example, step away from someone trying to hug you and shake your head to communicate "no."

- Send a text message to someone after an interaction explaining your boundaries and how they can respect them better next time.

Enforcing a boundary or self-advocating for better treatment should always be done in the way that is most direct for improved efficacy. Depending on who you're trying to communicate with, your approach may be different. For example, you may send an employer an email to discuss your boundaries but use words in person with a parent or partner.

However, you need to be careful here. Not everyone is safe enough to communicate rejection or discomfort with. If you feel this is the case or your communication is met with worsened behavior, skip straight to the final step of your strategy.

Step 4: Do Something

To fully self-advocate, you must take action to support your needs and boundaries. Along with communication, the action you take will promote real, lasting change in your relationships. This is especially important when someone does not want to respect your boundaries and does not respond well to your communication efforts. This is when you might need to:

- Leave the situation as quickly and safely as possible.
- Call for help from someone you trust or the authorities.
- Tell a loved one or therapist what's going on within the relationship.
- Carefully distance yourself from the person.
- Report malpractice if the situation involves a doctor or professional service provider.

It's important that you don't face dangerous or uncomfortable situations alone. Always take some form of action, even if that is just telling someone you trust that something happened. If the situation is minor, like a misunderstanding with a family member, the situation should be resolved easily. But if you notice that communicating your boundaries in a clear and respectful way escalates a situation, it may be a sign that the person involved does not have your best interest at heart.

Discerning people's intentions can be very difficult. However, I will always encourage you to trust your instincts and use the ABCD strategy to ensure you are being treated the way you deserve. People with bad intentions may be mistreating you in plain sight, and it might not always be obvious to others or even to you.

That's why you must question the intentions and behavior of others and take the necessary self-advocacy steps to stay safe in a world where the victimization of autistic people is so prevalent. Being able to self-advocate means standing up for yourself, even if you lose friends in the process. But this can be hard to do with the communication struggles that often come with autism. However, if you want to learn how to communicate effectively without losing your authenticity or hiding your autistic traits, you're going to have to turn the page to Chapter 9.

TOOL #7: AUTISTIC COMMUNICATION SKILLS

Building Connections And Confidence Without Losing Authenticity

"Autism is not a language barrier. It's a different language."

– Haley Moss

When I'm upset, I struggle to control my tone of voice. It can get out of hand if I don't actively manage it. There was a time when my tone of voice perpetuated an argument cycle within my romantic relationship.

He was very sensitive to the changes in my tone, even though they didn't accurately communicate my intentions. They reflected my intense emotions. But without adjusting them, a relationship that meant a lot to me became strained.

At the best of times, conversations take a lot of work. There's so much to stay aware of and manage. From monitoring eye contact, facial expressions, and body language to thinking about what you want to say and how you're supposed to say it without causing a misunderstanding. Neurotypical communication is not something that comes naturally for most autistic people.

But that doesn't mean we are bad communicators. We may communicate fluently with other neurodivergent people. You could say that we have a language of our own rather than a communication deficit. However, that's not to say we can't improve a couple of things. Most people, neurodivergent or not, could improve their communication skills. Autistic people may just have to approach it a little differently.

This is where I need to make a very clear distinction: there is a difference between learning to adjust your communication style and masking. This chapter is not going to encourage masking to any degree. Tool #7 is learning vital communication skills that can function within your autistic framework.

Authenticity is the greatest asset you can use to make fulfilling and long-lasting connections. This chapter is simply about finding ways to communicate your authentic self more accurately.

Much like my example, emotions can muddy communication. They can get in the way of what we are trying to say. When I realized the impact my emotions had on my communication style, everything changed. I could take a deep breath and purposefully adjust my tone to better reflect my intentions, and the argument would fizzle out immediately. It really was that simple.

Not always easy, but simple.

In this chapter, I'd like you to address your communication style and struggles so you can effectively apply the skills I'm going to teach you. Be prepared to try some new things that may feel uncomfortable at first but will blossom into beautiful connections and social confidence.

EMBRACING YOUR COMMUNICATION STYLE AND DIFFERENCES

Social deficits are some of the most common and significant autistic traits. They can include difficulties with communication, emotional expression, initiation, and maintenance. However, these deficits are in comparison to neurotypical communication and social norms. They do not reflect how well autistic people may connect and communicate with other autistic people.

With that said, I'd like you to think about your social well-being and consider which of the following aspects of communication you struggle with in relation to social norms:

- Nonverbal communication: Body language, personal space, eye contact, facial expressions, tone of voice, vocal volume, hand gestures, and speaking rhythm.

- Verbal communication: Choice of words, articulation, and ability to verbally communicate.

- Listening: Processing what you hear, focus, and understanding.

- Interpersonal communication: Joining in with a group, speaking at appropriate times, and initiating conversation.

It's important that you clarify your personal communication differences to experience a positive shift in your social connections. I don't want you to see them as flaws but rather as aspects of your communication style that you might want to improve or learn to work with. Take a moment now to go to your Workbook and complete the exercise waiting for you.

Treatment for social deficits has included therapies such as ABA, also known as applied behavioral analysis, a common and often highly recommended treatment option to reduce many autistic traits.[30]

However, while this treatment option aims to support autistic people in learning new skills, it is done in a way that often suppresses autistic traits for better social camouflage rather than encouraging working with autistic traits. It also spurs from questionable research and cruel experiments.[31]

The success reported for this therapy is mostly based on the effectiveness of skills learned and not the overall well-being of the individual. I say this because of the prevalence of PTSD symptoms in autistic adults who underwent successful ABA treatment as children.[32]

I don't want you to use the communication skills we are about to go through to suppress your traits or needs to fit in or appear to be functioning better. I want you to use these skills to genuinely improve your social experiences as your authentic autistic self. You may need to alter some behaviors, but only to better serve your ability to communicate your true self.

Many things can influence your behavior to communicate in a way that isn't true to you, such as anxiety, depression, and certain autistic traits. Let's take the necessary steps to let your authentic nature shine through and attract the people meant for you.

BUILDING AUTHENTIC CONNECTIONS WITH AUTISTIC COMMUNICATION SKILLS

Let's switch the focus from deficits and differences to skills and strengths. While many autistic people may have difficulties fitting communication norms, we have a unique set of communication strengths, too. Autistic communication skills lie in the areas of communication that come naturally to us.

For example, many autistic people are told that we are blunt and too honest, but that can be a positive thing! Being straightforward and honest are positive communication skills. They remove the need for others to read between the lines, and they make you a reliable source of information.

Or, what if you struggle to articulate yourself properly in conversation but can write beautiful poetry that captures the emotions of others? I would say that is a strength that many people could only dream of.

Whatever your communication style, you don't have to change it to be a better communicator; you simply have to work with it and ensure that the skills you do have convey your needs and intentions accurately.

The Key To Autistic Communication

The aspects of communication we covered before are only part of the equation. There are three more aspects of communication that are the key to communicating effectively as an autistic person. They include:

- Visual
- Written
- Intrapersonal

These three aspects of communication may be more valuable to focus on as they complement the commonly perceived deficits in autistic communication. Let's dive into each one and discuss how they might work better for you.

Visual

Visual communication is going to be the most important form of communication for autistic people who are nonverbal or experience selective mutism, a condition where you might lose the ability to speak during times of stress or conflict.

Visual communication includes tools such as graphs, pictures, and objects. It works well to supplement conversations and draw attention to your needs, ideas, and intentions. For example, you might explain your mood or energy levels using a mood chart or gesturing to a point on a graph. This can help others understand how you feel and respect your needs and boundaries appropriately.

Written

Written communication is a fantastic way to supplement conversations and ensure a more fulfilling experience. It can help you communicate fully if you are nonverbal or better articulate yourself in spoken conversations.

For example, you can use written communication in the form of texts, emails, or letters to ask for clarity about a situation, express your thoughts and emotions with more time to process them, and plan for what you would like to say in situations where emotions or distractions may interrupt you. This can include situations like doctor visits, business meetings, conflict resolution, and family discussions.

Intrapersonal

Intrapersonal communication refers to the communication that we have with ourselves. It's how often and how well we communicate with ourselves inside our minds. Although autistic people were thought to have a major deficit in self-awareness, studies show that our level of insight into ourselves is not much different from neurotypical people.[33]

It's actually more likely that neurodivergent people are more introspective because of our increased risk of isolation and introversion. Introversion can significantly increase your potential for greater self-awareness as it increases the amount of time you spend alone and in reflective mental states.[34]

Having a good relationship with yourself and improving your intrapersonal communication can help you in a number of important ways. It can help you:

- Better understand yourself and your needs.
- Form a better relationship with yourself to improve confidence levels.
- Nurture a more compassionate inner voice for a more encouraging social experience.
- Reflect on social experiences and notice where you could have improved.
- Identify and regulate your emotions more readily.

Having a deeper sense of self-awareness is the ultimate tool for better communication. Without self-awareness, it's very difficult to see where you might go wrong and apply strategies for improved communication.

As an autistic adult, you might naturally have formed a deeper sense of self-awareness through facing and questioning the many social difficulties common to your experience. Your self-awareness will also have increased and will continue to increase as you stick to using the tools you learn in this book.

For example, journaling, somatic practice, mindfulness, and learning to self-advocate will all increase your self-awareness. They all require you to reflect extensively on your life, behaviors, and struggles. Self-reflection is the path to self-awareness.

Steps To Better Overall Communication

Now that you've considered your communication differences and strengths let's discuss ways to improve your overall communication skills. The goal of good communication is to accurately communicate what is going on inside your body and mind and accurately interpret what others are communicating to you.

To achieve this goal, you can apply the following steps to your current communication style:

Step 1: Emotionally Regulate

Intense emotions can hinder clear communication. You may say something you don't mean, speak or behave in a way that doesn't reflect your true intentions, or become hindered by the intensity.

Miscommunications can cause significant problems in otherwise healthy relationships, so it's best to avoid them if possible.

Regulating your emotions can help you communicate in a more effective and true way. The good news is that you already have the tools to do it. You can regulate your emotions by:

- Calming and identifying them through somatic practice.
- Journaling about them to either clear them or understand them.
- Doing something you enjoy before expressing how you feel.

You can find ways to use these practices either before or during a conversation. For example, if you're in the middle of a conversation and feel an intense emotion come up, you can take a deep breath, ground yourself, and even excuse yourself for a moment. It's better to noticeably regulate an emotion or leave the situation than to let an intense emotion cause you to behave out of character. You can always come back to it when you're feeling clearer or via a text message.

Step 2: Express Empathy

Empathy comes in many forms, including the kind that you feel for others and the kind that you show others. I don't doubt that you experience empathy for others, but learning to express it properly can transform your relationships.

The kind of empathy that really impacts people is the kind that pays attention to what people respond to and adjusts to communicate care in a way that *they* will understand.

For example, if you hate hugs but someone continues to hug you in times of stress, their empathy might not come across as they intended. But if that same person adjusts their display of empathy to meet your needs it means so much more.

To express empathy in a way that makes the most impact on the people you care about, try to notice what comforts them in times of stress. Then, when you notice that person having a bad day, let your empathy shine through in a way you know they'll understand.

True empathy, which you not only feel but also express in a way that shows, is the kind that can quickly win friends and deepen connections.

Step 3: Be Open And Honest

Making connections that feel fulfilling and comfortable for you shouldn't require you to suppress your needs or overstep your boundaries. However, you may encounter many people who won't understand your needs and who may even misinterpret your behavior.

This is where I want you to remember your ABCD self-advocacy strategy from Chapter 8. Most importantly, you need to be able to communicate your needs and boundaries. These will be important to explain in conversation, especially with receptive neurotypical people.

For example, if you find eye contact extremely uncomfortable, don't force it. Rather, communicate your discomfort with eye contact to make it clear that your lack of eye contact is not a response to them. Always be open and honest about your needs and boundaries, even if others don't understand.

Step 4: Improve Nonverbal Communication

Nonverbal communication includes all the ways that we use our bodies to communicate, including our tone of voice and rhythm. It can account for up to 93% of in person communication.[35] You might send nonverbal messages on purpose, or completely by accident. What's important is that our bodies can communicate a lot of information without needing to say a word.

What's great about nonverbal communication is that you can use it to better understand someone's intentions. You can also use it to purposefully communicate something, like an emotion or statement, with your body alone.

For example, if you want someone to know that you're listening, you might adjust the direction of your shoulders toward them and encourage them. If you want someone to give you space, you can lift your palms at them, bringing your hands between you and them. If you notice that someone seems anxious and unsure, you can use a friendly facial expression with a smile to reveal your good intentions.

Understanding nonverbal communication comes from observing others and learning what certain cues mean. You can observe how good friends interact with each other, how someone's body changes when they become stressed or upset, and even the way people's faces express emotion.

To practice your nonverbal communication cues, try this simple and fun mirror exercise. All you need is a mirror, your imagination, and some privacy. Stand in front of the mirror and imagine different scenarios featuring different intentions and emotions.

See how your face and body change, and consider whether they are communicating accurately. Play around and experiment with different facial expressions, tones of voice, and other body language like gestures and posture.

Improving your nonverbal communication skills is not about putting on a mask. It's about becoming comfortable expressing yourself more accurately with your body. Use it to better communicate your thoughts, emotions, and intentions, not to hide them.

Step 5: Communicate With The Right People

You can have all the best intentions and the right communication skills, but if someone is not receptive to you, it still won't go well. This is where *who* you communicate with is important. Some signs that someone is not receptive to your communication efforts may include:

- Avoidance behaviors like stepping away from you, ignoring you, or avoiding being around you.

- Disinterested body language like turning their shoulders away from you, avoiding eye contact when eye contact isn't an issue for them, or folding their arms.

- Negative facial expressions like frowning, rolling their eyes, or looking unhappy and bored.

- Latching onto distractions such as looking relieved to see a friend of theirs so they can get up and leave, receiving a phone call and taking it right away, or checking messages while you're talking.

- Minimal responses like only giving one-word answers or responses to what you're saying and not asking any follow-up questions to engage in the topic.

Of course, these behaviors are not necessarily an indication that they don't like you. They may also just be having a bad day, experiencing anxiety, or struggling with communication difficulties. If you're unsure about how someone feels, apply your ABCD self-advocacy strategy here, too.

Ask yourself questions about the person's behavior, make sure that you feel comfortable and that your boundaries aren't being overstepped, communicate your concern if you feel safe to do so, and if you receive any indication that they are not treating you well, make sure to do something about it.

You will notice the difference between the right people to communicate with and the wrong ones. Some things you may experience when around someone receptive to your communication include:

- Feeling comfortable continuing to talk freely.
- Noticing your body language ease and open up.
- Feeling comfortable to be yourself and unmask more.
- Noticing signs of ease and comfort in them as well.
- A sense that the interaction is uplifting and positive.
- Receiving invites to spend time together again.
- Noticing someone make the effort to approach you.

- Feelings of fulfillment and joy after a connection forms.
- Noticing a lasting improvement in your wellbeing since knowing the person.

Remember to practice discernment, even when you think the person you're speaking to is receptive to communication. Not all people have good intentions, even when they appear kind. You will know the difference between someone who is genuine or not by noticing how they interact with others and paying attention to the long-term impact they have on you. The impact should always be positive and not contribute to your stress.

As autistic people, we will likely have unique ways of communicating, and there's nothing wrong with that. If you know what makes your communication style different, you can work with it to better express yourself and make connections.

However, making connections isn't always easy, even for the most well-connected neurotypical people. But there is a way to bypass the struggle of trying to connect with people who don't and simply won't want to "get you."

Connecting isn't always about being bad at socializing but rather about trying to socialize with the wrong people. If you're ready to put your communication skills to good use in places where you're sure to find weird and wonderful people just like you, then turn the page to the final tool in this book and get ready to immerse yourself in the autistic community and culture.

10

TOOL #8: DISCOVER YOUR SENSE OF BELONGING

The Power Of Connecting Within The Autistic Community

"Human connection is the most vital aspect of our existence. Without the sweet touch of another being, we are lonely stars in an empty space waiting to shine gloriously."

– Joe Straynge

Imagine a beautiful dolphin swimming and glistening in the shallow ocean waves. She is so clearly made for the water you wouldn't expect her ever to question that. However, below the surface, schools of fish swim together in unison, never seeming to need a break.

The dolphin wonders where she belongs. She wonders why, with each golden sunset, she can't resist breaking through the waves to see the awe-inspiring glow. She can't understand how the fish can hold their breath for so long when, at the same time underwater, it is suffocating for her.

The dolphin is different. And when she sees the fish working together so easily under the water, she doesn't know if she belongs there at all.

Like the dolphin, you might be comparing yourself to the perfectly functioning schools of fish all around you. You might see the structure of basic society and the lives of everyday adults successfully managing work, finances, family, and more. You might compare yourself to them and wonder why that life feels so suffocating for you.

But you are a dolphin. You are different in the way that you move through life. You see the world through eyes that might notice details others overlook. You don't only want to take time to break the surface for more play and rest, but you *need* to.

The thing about dolphins is they may not swim in schools, but they do have pods. They are never alone in the wild ocean waters. And when they find each other, they are powerful, happy, and vibrant beings. The same applies to you.

It's time to stop searching for connection and belonging in places where you don't connect, and you feel you don't belong. Tool #8 is your sense of belonging. To discover it, you're going to have to break the surface and find your pod. So, let's discuss the power of making connections within the autistic community and creative ways to expand your social circle.

THE AUTISTIC COMMUNITY

Studies show that autistic people make up only 1% of the world's population, but with improved diagnostic criteria and access, this percentage is growing.[36] Even so, this statistic might make you think that our community is small and not significant enough to find a sense of belonging within it. But 1% of the population still amounts to over 75 million people.

In today's modern society, we have the luxury of being able to connect via the internet. Much of the autistic adult community is online, connecting in places like the comments sections of autistic content, social media, and online communities with thousands of members.

The climate of the online autistic community has proven to be little less than supportive, understanding, and willing to help. The internet is a place where our 1% can come together, share experiences, and feel seen. It's a place where I will encourage you to get comfortable in a safe and beneficial way. It shouldn't be the only place where you connect with others, but it can be rewarding when used properly.

In this chapter, we will discuss some safe places, both online and in person, to connect with other autistic people. But for now, there's a very important question we need to address: Why don't you belong? Or rather, why is it that autistic people often struggle with belonging?

WHY DON'T YOU BELONG?

There is a growing body of research that suggests autistic social deficits are bidirectional, meaning that the struggles we face socially in a neurotypical world are not because we are bad at communicating but rather because there is an acute level of misunderstanding between people of different neurotypes.[37]

The studies actually indicate that autistic socializing issues are more connected to being misunderstood than communicating "poorly." This comes from witnessing how well autistic people can often communicate with each other. So, as we discussed at the end of the previous chapter, *who* you spend time with will determine how comfortable you feel socializing.

This is where I need you to address your current sense of belonging and determine why you might feel isolated. Even if you don't feel this way all the time, it's a common struggle within our community, and it's worth having a strategy in place if it does occur.

Addressing Your Sense Of Belonging

Take this as an opportunity to analyze your social life and all the connections you may already have. Many of your close connections, like family and friends, will form part of your support system, a vital component of well-being. If your support system isn't satisfying your need for connection, it may need to expand.

Taking a good look at how your support system functions can help you understand why you might feel so alienated or alone at times. It can also reveal where there's room for improvement.

When you're ready, head to your Workbook and use the questions waiting for you to gain valuable insight into your current sense of belonging and social fulfillment. These questions include:

- Does your social life feel fulfilling and healthy?
- How often do you spend time with others and have a good time?
- Who do you spend the most time with in any given month?
- Are there other neurodivergent people in your social circle?
- When you have a problem, who can you talk to about it?
- Do you feel understood by the people you spend the most time with?
- Can you be yourself around your closest friends and family?

It's important to know, no matter how misunderstood you might feel, that there are people out there just like you, hoping to make connections, too.

The reason why autistic people struggle socially has a lot to do with living in a world that puts pressure on the "right" way to do

Tool #8: Discover Your Sense Of Belonging

things like function, socialize, and communicate. But thriving as an autistic adult takes authenticity. That might mean doing things the "wrong" way, or rather in ways that are different from the norm but which absolutely work for you.

The great thing about being authentic is that the connections you make are more likely to last and feel fulfilling. Your willingness to embrace, love, and be yourself will bring the right people into your life. These people can include those you simply have a good time with and people who make their way into your support system.

Let's explore the many ways that you can attract great relationships without having to mask or fit in.

FINDING YOUR POD

It's possible to find connections anywhere there are people, but I'd like you to start within the autistic community and work your way out from there. Connections can come in many forms. They may be friends, acquaintances, romantic relationships, or role models. The important thing is that they make you feel seen, understood, and like you belong.

Like the dolphin, I'd like you to focus on finding your pod—people just like you. Even if that is just one person for now, it'll make a big difference and encourage you to keep expanding your social circle.

Humans are, by nature, social creatures.[38] Even if you are someone who prefers to have a very small social circle, like me, a healthy social circle is important for living your best life. Some fun and exciting ways to meet other neurodivergent people and improve the quality of your social life include:

Join Autistic Led Communities And Groups

Search for any autistic communities or groups, both local and online. Check that autistic people run the communities or groups you join to ensure that you are in a safe space to be yourself and make authentic connections. You can do this by checking the online group guidelines or asking the admins and organizers.

If you're unsure, join the group and experience it for yourself. If you don't feel comfortable somewhere or feel misunderstood within the community, don't give up. Not all groups and communities are made equal, so keep trying until you find one that works for you.

However, I can guarantee safety, acceptance, and inclusivity in the LearnWell Community.

Join In-Person Events For The Autistic Community

Depending on where you live, there may be in-person events and meetups organized for the autistic community. These may include autism awareness campaigns, social meetups, or other inclusive events. If you're nervous about attending an in-person event alone, ask someone you trust, like a friend or family member, to go with you.

Some events might also attract the kinds of people you'd like to be around, such as comic conventions or other conventions related to your interests. Chances are, you might not be the only autistic person present whose special interest correlates with the event.

Find People You Enjoy Being Around Through Hobbies And Interests

Like-minded people may not always be neurodivergent. Sometimes, what's important is finding people you enjoy being around. This can include people with similar interests or the kinds of people you generally like. Take a moment now to consider what type of person you are and what type of person you prefer to spend time with.

For example, are you outgoing and energetic, or are you more quiet? Do you prefer people with a lot of energy, or do you prefer people who can peacefully sit and relax with you? Depending on your preferences, you can spend time in places that generally attract the kinds of people you like. Combine that with an interest or hobby, and you will have a recipe for making friends. For example:

- If you love nature and would enjoy friends who are energetic, you can join a hiking group.

- Maybe you love to get creative and would prefer friends who are more peaceful. In this case, you could join an art or pottery class.

- If you are talkative and love to read, join a book club that encourages lots of social banter.

- Perhaps you are only relaxed around animals and would prefer friends who feel the same. Try going to places with petting zoos or taking up a hobby that involves animals, like horse-riding or bee-keeping.

When you're looking for like-minded people and hoping to meet them spontaneously during social activities, you might be surprised that the people you connect best with are neurodivergent anyway. It's not a must, but it's definitely a bonus!

Start A Club For Neurodiverse Folk In Your Area

If you'd like to meet other neurodivergent people but there aren't any clubs or groups in your area, start one! There are many popular and safe ways to start a regular opportunity for neurodiverse folk to meet, including:

- Book clubs
- Walking groups
- Park meetups
- Monthly theatre dates
- Craft clubs

Choose a meetup idea that you feel comfortable with, and start spreading the word via social media, flyers, and word of mouth. Even if it starts with just you and a family member, keep up with the routine of meeting in a set place and time and let new connections come to you!

Reconnect With Old Like-Minded Friends

Adult lives get busy, and it's only natural for friendships to ebb and flow. If there is someone you really enjoyed being friends with, but the two of you drifted apart, maybe it's time to rekindle the friendship. It can be as simple as reconnecting via social media or sending a message to see how they're doing. If they're receptive to it, see how it goes. You might have a great connection already waiting in your contacts list.

Of course, practice caution if the friendship ends badly. However, know that it's not uncommon for any friendship to include the occasional misunderstanding. If you feel that the friendship was good but ended prematurely, maybe making up is worthwhile.

There are many things that make up a life of thriving. For autistic people, that includes learning to be yourself, improving your emotional regulation, self-advocating, and more. However, a healthy support system is just as important. That means having friends, family, and role models that make you feel seen and understood.

Without a healthy support system, your sense of belonging will be impacted. A sense of belonging helps you feel stable in the rough waters of life. It makes both the good and the bad times better. And it reminds you that you are perfectly lovable, exactly the way you are. Sometimes, it just takes the right people to help you confirm that.

Life is not meant to be lived alone. Even with all the powerful ways that you can and will support yourself, make sure you find others who will support you, too. Whether it's autistic strangers on the internet or autistic creators such as myself, the autistic community is here, and we're here to support you. When you're ready, meet me on the next and final page. There's one last thing I'd like to say.

CONCLUSION

Your commitment to reading this book and applying the lessons within it is already showing. It makes me so proud to share something in common with you that influences our lives in such a profound way. However, I want to acknowledge that I know it doesn't come without some significant difficulties.

I hope that this book has impacted you and encouraged you to keep going and try new ways to live your best, most vibrant life. If there comes a time, however soon or far, when you feel lost or in need of more support, please come back to this book and use it as an ongoing resource. In it you will rediscover your 8 tools for autistic thriving:

1. Somatic practice as a form of stimming.
2. Self-accommodations you can make.
3. Autistic joy through special interests and hobbies.
4. Keeping a journal to express and learn more about yourself.
5. Managing executive dysfunction with more play and rewards.
6. The ABCD self-advocacy strategy for safer, more respectful relationships.
7. Autistic communication skills for more fulfilling social interactions.
8. Finding your sense of belonging within the autistic community.

Tool #8: Discover Your Sense Of Belonging

You should know that I've never felt more connected to my reader than I have throughout this book. We are connected by our neurodiversity, and it's a connection we will keep for the rest of our lives.

Knowing that, I hope that you feel a little less alone. May that allow you to feel a little closer to home and bring you a sense of comfort you might not have had before.

I see you, and you've now seen me.

Thank you for being here,

Rose.

REFERENCES

1. https://www.nimh.nih.gov/health/topics/autism-spectrum-disorders-asd#:~:text=Autism%20spectrum%20disorder%20(ASD)%20is,communicate%2C%20learn%2C%20and%20behave
2. https://www.ncbi.nlm.nih.gov/pmc/articles/PMC2661453/
3. https://www.ncbi.nlm.nih.gov/pmc/articles/PMC9804307/#:~:text=Many%20studies%20show%20that%20autistic,Baron%E2%80%90Cohen%2C%202013
4. https://www.rcpsych.ac.uk/docs/default-source/improving-care/nccmh/suicide-prevention/workshops-(wave-4)/wave-4-workshop-2/suicide-and-autism---slides.pdf?sfvrsn=bf3e0113_2
5. https://www.washington.edu/doit/what-do-%E2%80%9Cneurodiverse%E2%80%9D-and-%E2%80%9Cneurodivergent%E2%80%9D-mean
6. https://nurselinecs.co.uk/autism/the-impact-of-autism-masking-on-mental-health/
7. https://www.accessliving.org/newsroom/blog/ableism-101/
8. https://www.ncbi.nlm.nih.gov/pmc/articles/PMC6728747/#:~:text=Autistic%20adults%20highlighted%20the%20importance,aims%20to%20eliminate%20the%20behaviour
9. https://autism.org/webinars/how-the-autonomic-nervous-system-may-govern-anxiety-in-autism/
10. https://www.ambitiousaboutautism.org.uk/information-about-autism/behaviour/meltdowns-and-shutdowns
11. https://www.ncbi.nlm.nih.gov/pmc/articles/PMC3010743/

References

12. https://www.frontiersin.org/articles/10.3389/fninf.2013.00037/full
13. https://www.ncbi.nlm.nih.gov/pmc/articles/PMC3754787/#:~:text=Several%20authors%20have%20reported%20on,matching%20proprioception%20with%20vision%20during
14. https://bond.edu.au/news/humming-healthy-mmm-heres-what-evidence-says
15. https://autismspectrumnews.org/the-prevalence-of-comorbidities-in-autism-consideration-of-comorbidity-in-intervention-and-treatment-response/
16. https://www.ncbi.nlm.nih.gov/pmc/articles/PMC7445808/
17. https://www.health.harvard.edu/blog/how-can-you-find-joy-or-at-least-peace-during-difficult-times-202210062826#:~:text=Surprising%20benefits%20of%20joy&text=Your%20immune%20system%20can%20be,can%20help%20you%20live%20longer
18. https://www.cambridge.org/core/journals/advances-in-psychiatric-treatment/article/emotional-and-physical-health-benefits-of-expressive-writing/ED2976A61F5DE56B46F07A1CE9EA9F9F
19. https://www.ncbi.nlm.nih.gov/pmc/articles/PMC6220635/
20. https://www.ncbi.nlm.nih.gov/pmc/articles/PMC4402011/
21. https://ggia.berkeley.edu/practice/expressive_writing
22. https://www.uclahealth.org/news/health-benefits-gratitude
23. https://www.additudemag.com/what-is-executive-function-disorder/
24. https://autisticandunapologetic.com/2020/02/23/autism-exploitation-how-to-spot-it-and-how-to-make-it-stop/
25. https://emergentdivergence.com/2021/09/29/creating-autistic-suffering-in-the-beginning-there-was-trauma/

26. https://www.ncbi.nlm.nih.gov/pmc/articles/PMC5886362/
27. https://autism.org/sexual-victimization-in-autism/#:~:text=Autistic%20youth%20are%20three%20to,Weiss%20%26%20Fardella%2C%202018
28. https://pubmed.ncbi.nlm.nih.gov/35524162/
29. https://www.sciencedaily.com/releases/2018/05/180522114817.htm
30. https://www.ncbi.nlm.nih.gov/pmc/articles/PMC9084456/
31. https://blogs.uoregon.edu/autismhistoryproject/topics/applied-behavior-analysis/
32. https://www.psychologytoday.com/intl/blog/nurturing-self-esteem-in-autistic-children/202209/does-applied-behavior-analysis-aba-cause
33. https://www.ncbi.nlm.nih.gov/pmc/articles/PMC4122539/
34. https://www.health.com/introvert-7480695#:~:text=Self%2Dawareness%3A%20Introverts%20are%20often,and%20improve%20in%20the%20future
35. https://www.ncbi.nlm.nih.gov/pmc/articles/PMC6127604/
36. https://www.who.int/news-room/fact-sheets/detail/autism-spectrum-disorders
37. https://www.ncbi.nlm.nih.gov/pmc/articles/PMC8114326/
38. https://www.ncbi.nlm.nih.gov/pmc/articles/PMC2527715/

www.ingramcontent.com/pod-product-compliance
Lightning Source LLC
Chambersburg PA
CBHW071208070526
44584CB00019B/2959